"Steve Monsma avoids the modern-day tendency to believe that the kingdom of God will arrive on Air Force One. Instead he offers a balanced, thoughtful perspective on how Christians should engage in the political process. His solid biblical grounding, as well as his concrete applications of Christian principles to public policy, provides wise guidance."

—CHARLES W. COLSON, Prison Fellowship

"Urgent, compelling, readable. An important book on a crucial topic. Monsma's entire life—as a successful politician and a gifted professor of political science—has prepared him to write this clear, compelling book. Every Christian with any interest in politics should read it."

—RONALD J. SIDER, Evangelicals for Social Action

"If you need to know in advance whether the author is a conservative or a liberal, you may not like Monsma's approach. He asks you to set aside such simplistic labels and go back and ask instead what the Bible says about each of a dozen key public policy issues. And then if you disagree with some of his personal conclusions—just as he expects you to—you will always appreciate his candor and honesty. This is a thinking person's book."

—JOEL BELZ, Founder, *World Magazine*

"Wise, helpful, and comprehensive, *Healing for a Broken World* shows the way for a Christian engagement with politics that is constructive. If it had been read thirty years ago, it would have saved us from all the excesses of the religious right that are creating such a backlash today."

—OS GUINNESS, author of *Unspeakable: Facing up to the Challenge of Evil*

"Monsma hit a home run just at the time evangelicals need to reassess the assumptions on which we voice our views on a whole range of critical issues."

—ROBERT ANDRINGA, President Emeritus,
Council of Christian Colleges and Universities

"This is an important introduction to issues arising at the intersection of faith and politics, written from a disciplined Kuyperism/Calvinist theoretical stance and resulting in a nuanced centrist evangelical perspective. The book is reader-friendly, biblical, holistic, and wise. Monsma's wide experience and excellent research make this a quite valuable resource."

—DAVID GUSHEE, Graves Professor of Moral Philosophy, Union University

"If believers will read this book—or better yet, discuss it in groups—there's a strong possibility a fresh Christian chorus may be heard in the land. It is my hope that believers will read, ponder, and discuss."

—JUDSON POLING, Willow Creek Community Church

"An essential guidebook for evanglicals seeking to navigate the complexity of faith and public life while remaining grounded in their faith. For people of all faiths and persuasions, this book is a valuable resource for understanding the history and depth of evangelical thinking about the public square."

—REV. JENNIFER BUTLER, Executive Director, Faith in Public Life

"Monsma is one of the most important scholars writing on church-state issues today. This latest contribution is perhaps his finest work. It brings together his wide-ranging knowledge of the history of politics and jurisprudence with a theological seriousness that is often lacking in much church-state scholarship. For Monsma, Christian theology is a knowledge tradition, not simply private piety that has its rightful place only in a sequestered sphere from which it cannot count against the deliverances of so-called 'secular reason.' On the other hand, Monsma is a thoughtful defender of religious liberty and liberal democracy as necessary bulwarks that help protect the rights of Christians and non-Christians alike. Thus, this book should be in the hands of anyone who takes theology and politics seriously."

—FRANCIS J. BECKWITH,
Associate Professor of Philosophy and Church-State Studies, Baylor University

"Monsma calls evangelicals to careful thinking about our political responsibilities. This book requires a careful reading by any Christian who is seriously committed to engaging their mind, heart, and strength to the world of politics and government. But be warned. Monsma will challenge you to re-think assumptions about political ideology, power, tactics, and the emphasis on charisma in American political life. He takes the reader back to the basic biblical premise that Christians must be committed to justice for all—believer or not—for the sake of Christ's kingdom, rather than for the construction of some idealized political or economic society."

—RON MAHURIN, VP for Professional Development & Research,
Council of Christian Colleges and Universities

"Politics can be a perilous subject to tackle in the church, but this book offers a way to deal with important concepts in a mature and healthy way. This is the ideal resource for a church or small group wanting to explore what it looks like to be faithful citizens."

—JASON POLING, Senior Pastor, Our New Hope Community

HEALING FOR
A BROKEN
WORLD

CHRISTIAN PERSPECTIVES
ON PUBLIC POLICY

STEVE MONSMA

WHEATON, ILLINOIS

Healing for a Broken World: Christian Perspectives on Public Policy

Copyright © 2008 by Steve Monsma

Published by Crossway
          1300 Crescent Street
          Wheaton, Illinois 60187

Interior design and typesetting by Lakeside Design Plus

Cover design: Cindy Kiple

First printing 2008

Printed in the United States of America

Unless otherwise indicated, Scripture references are from *The Holy Bible: New International Version*®. Copyright © 1973, 1978, 1984 by International Bible Society. Used by permission of Zondervan Publishing House. All rights reserved.

The "NIV" and "New International Version" trademarks are registered in the United States Patent and Trademark Office by International Bible Society. Use of either trademark requires the permission of International Bible Society.

Scripture quotations marked TNIV are taken from *The Holy Bible, Today's New International Version*®. TNIV®. Copyright © 2001, 2005 by International Bible Society. Used by permission of Zondervan. All rights reserved.

Scripture quotations marked KJV are from the *King James Version* of the Bible.

All emphases in Scripture quotations have been added by the author.

ISBN-13: 978-1-58134-961-0
ISBN-10: 1-58134-961-0
ePub ISBN: 978-1-4335-2124-9
PDF ISBN: 978-1-4335-0311-5
Mobipocket ISBN: 978-1-4335-0652-9

Library of Congress Cataloging-in-Publication Data
Monsma, Stephen V., 1936–
   Healing for a broken world : Christian perspectives on public
policy / Steve Monsma.
      p. cm.
   Includes bibliographical references and index.
   ISBN 978-1-58134-961-0 (tpb)
   1. Christianity and politics. 2. Public policy. I. Title.
BR115.P7M555   2007
261.7—dc22   2007027985

Crossway is a publishing ministry of Good News Publishers.
AM   24 23 22 21 20 19 18 17 16 15 14

To my grandchildren,

Caitlin Elizabeth Flanagan

and

William Carlisle Flanagan

Contents

Preface

EVANGELICALS ARE TODAY A MAJOR FORCE on the American political scene. We make up one-fourth to one-third of all voters. Our leaders are invited to the White House. Every election politicians appeal to us for our votes. We are quoted on CNN and find ourselves on the front pages of the *New York Times*.

But for many evangelicals, myself included, this heightened influence and attention generates more dismay than rejoicing. Too often our voices are shrill, our grasp of the facts thin, and our vision narrow. Our leaders often embarrass the rest of us with their strident voices and cocksure positions.

The religious left seems to offer no more than warmed-over versions of the tired positions of the Democratic left; the religious right seems to do the same for the tired positions of the Republican right.

We evangelicals are rightly known for our efforts to bring the good news of Jesus Christ to the lost at home and around the world, to explore boldly new forms of worship and new church structures, and increasingly to create agencies to care for the needy in our communities and abroad. Our churches are full and our agencies vigorous. But are we ready to follow the call of Scripture to be good citizens? Do we know how to be not simply good citizens, but good *Christian* citizens?

This book is for people who want to answer the call to be good Christian citizens but are uncertain what this means in today's world. It goes back to basics: to Scripture and key biblical principles relevant to our lives as Christian citizens. It then applies these principles to specific public-policy questions that are daily in the news.

It does not attempt to give a simple, supposedly "Christian," answer to every public-policy question—and then make one feel guilty if one does not immediately embrace it. We have had too much of that. Instead, its goal is to help Christians understand basic biblical principles and then use them to live as thoughtful, conscientious citizens.

Different Christians, equally thoughtful and equally committed to following God's Word, will sometimes reach different conclusions. But that is OK. The truly important thing is that we approach public-policy issues humbly and with our minds shaped by biblically-based principles, not by the various political idols of our day.

It is my deepest prayer that this book will be used by God to help us evangelicals as citizens to be more faithful to him and his Word. As we are, we will be prepared to be used by God to be salt and light in our communities, our nation, and our world.

When the Jews in exile in Persia were threatened with destruction, Mordecai urged Esther the queen to take action with these words: "Who knows but that you have come to royal position for such a time as this?" (Est. 4:14). As citizens in a free, democratic country, we evangelicals also have the potential for great influence. Paraphrasing Mordecai, "Who knows but that we have come to a position of great influence in the world's most powerful nation for such a time as this?"

In writing this book I had the help from many persons along the way. I owe all of them a large debt of gratitude. I begin by thanking editors Allan Fisher and Tara Davis, whose support, suggestions, and editorial revisions have strengthened this book. Also, in the early stages of my thinking through this project five people encouraged me to proceed with it and offered key suggestions: Stanley Carlson-Thies, Richard Cizik, Luis Lugo, Ronald Sider, and James Skillen.

A group of sixteen evangelical church leaders, academics, and public policy advocates agreed to serve as a task force of consultants for this book. We met in Washington, D.C., for a full day of meetings, and they responded to my email enquiries and updates with helpful comments and suggestions. In addition to Richard Cizik, James Skillen, and Ronald Sider, this task force of consultants consisted of

Jennifer Butler, Danny Cortes, Michael Cromartie, Keith Hill, Joe Loconte, Dan Meyer, John Northrup, Jason Poling, Judson Poling, Corwin Smidt, Harold Dean Trulear, and David Worth. I owe each of these persons a public acknowledgment for their help. Among them, I owe a special thanks to Jason Poling, pastor of Our New Hope Community Church in Baltimore, who read the entire manuscript carefully and offered many helpful, sometimes frank, ego-bruising suggestions. The book is a more readable book that is also more faithful to Scripture because of his help.

I also wish to thank the Paul B. Henry Institute for the Study of Christianity and Politics and its director, Corwin Smidt, for their support. The Institute funded the meeting of the task force and in numerous other ways supported the writing of this book. I also wish to thank my colleagues at Calvin College in both political science and communications. They were invariably generous in their suggestions and words of encouragement. A special word of thanks to one of my colleagues, Amy Patterson, who helped with factual information and insights for chapter 11 on challenges Africa is facing today.

In the same breath as my thanks I must make clear that the fault for any errors that remain in this book and any insights that are less than accurate or less than scriptural remain mine alone. Please do not blame those who helped me for any shortcomings in this book.

Lastly, I dedicate this book to Caitlin Elizabeth and William Carlisle Flanagan, my grandchildren, with the prayer that they will inherit a world more fully redeemed in all its aspects than what it is today, and that one day they too may take their places as followers of Jesus Christ who are used by him to help heal a world that is all too often still broken.

Steve Monsma
August, 2007

1

Our Starting Point:

*"Take Captive Every Thought
to Make It Obedient to Christ"*

(2   C o r i n t h i a n s   1 0 : 5)

IN 1785 THE ENGLISH ECONOMY was largely built on the slave trade, the cruelly exploitive policies of the East India Company toward India, and laborers, even children, who worked long hours in mines and factories under brutal conditions. The government was dominated by a corrupt elite class addicted to its privileges and a status-conscious social whirl. It was also the year that God called a twenty-six-year-old member of Parliament, William Wilberforce, out of a life of privilege and fashionable entertainments; in part through the witness of John Newton, a former slave trader and evangelist, William Wilberforce was convicted of his sin, turned to Jesus Christ as his Savior, and began a life-long commitment to serving him.[1]

Wilberforce considered leaving his political career, but Newton persuaded him to stay in Parliament and use his position to influence England for the good. He urged Wilberforce with these words: "God has raised you up for the good of the church and the good of the nation, maintain your friendship with Pitt [the prime minister], continue in Parliament, who knows that but for such a time as this

God has brought you into public life and has a purpose for you."[2]
Over the next forty-eight years, God used Wilberforce and other
evangelicals who gathered around him for enormous good. They
ended the British slave trade, won the freedom of all slaves in British
territories, changed British policy toward India in a more humane
direction, and worked for reforms in education, health care, child
labor, and the prisons.

The role Wilberforce played in the abolition of the slave trade and
later in slavery itself was powerfully pictured in the 2007 feature film
Amazing Grace. The film makes
clear that the faith of Wilberforce was not a private affair that
touched only his personal and
spiritual life; it was a blazing fire
that transformed his entire life,
including his political career. As
a result God used him to change
Britain—and the world.

Why was God able to use Wilberforce to accomplish much
good? Five characteristics marked
Wilberforce's action as a public
figure. We can still learn from
them today. First, Wilberforce
had a deep, personal commitment
to Jesus Christ that transformed
all aspects of his life. Christ was
at the center of his life. This commitment deeply affected his work
as a member of Parliament. And it did not stop there. He founded
the British Bible Society and was active in organizations to prevent
cruelty to animals. He regularly gave away large portions of his income to a variety of charities. His commitment to Jesus Christ as his
Savior, his work as a member of Parliament, and his work in missionary and other reform organizations—all three—were cut from the
same piece of cloth. And that cloth was his devotion to Jesus Christ.
He was not a politician who thought all the answers to society's ills
would come through changing public policies; nor was he a devout
believer who thought his Christian duty ended with cultivating an

"It was the faithful, persistent and
enduring enthusiasm of . . . William
Wilberforce . . . and [his] noble
co-workers, that finally thawed the
British heart into sympathy for the
slave, and moved the strong arm of
that government in mercy to put an
end to his bondage. Let no
American, especially no colored
American, withhold a generous
recognition of this stupendous
achievement."[3]

—FREDERICK DOUGLASS,
NINETEENTH-CENTURY FREED AMERICAN
SLAVE AND ABOLITIONIST

inner life of devotion to Christ. Jesus Christ claimed and transformed his entire life.

A second characteristic that marked Wilberforce's efforts in public life was that he did not act alone, but was part of a group of fellow Christians who prayed, planned, and worked together. Many of them purposely lived near each other in the Clapham section of greater London and came to be known as the Clapham group.

A third mark of Wilberforce's efforts in public life was the great opposition—even derision and death threats—that he and his fellow evangelicals faced during their long, drawn-out struggles for reform. The slave-owning plantation owners in the West Indies, the slave traders, and great seaports such as Liverpool bitterly opposed the ending of the highly lucrative slave trade. Many, in fact, saw it as a mainstay of the British economy. It took over twenty years, and failure after failure, before they succeeded in ending the British slave trade, and only as Wilberforce lay dying, in

> "Wilberforce should be an inspiration to every person of faith who takes seriously the obligation, responsibility and commission to make a difference in society."[4]
>
> —RICHARD LAND, PRESIDENT, SOUTHERN BAPTIST ETHICS AND RELIGIOUS LIBERTY COMMISSION

1833, did the British House of Commons vote to end slavery in all its territories. The British East India Company bitterly opposed efforts to reform exploitive British practices toward India, and it took years of struggle and several defeats in Parliament before Wilberforce and his fellow evangelicals in 1813 won passage of key reforms.

Fourth, Wilberforce and his fellow Clapham reformers worked for the greater good of society as a whole. They were not, as an evangelical special-interest group, out to protect the narrow self-interests of their fellow believers or their social class. They sought the common good, not their own welfare. Wilberforce and almost all in the Clapham group were people of wealth and social standing. Yet time and again they took on the causes of the poorest and least of their day. The Africans, who were the victims of the unimaginably cruel practices of the slave traders, were not fellow Christian believers and were totally dispossessed with no legal rights at all. Nevertheless, Wilberforce and his coworkers labored for over twenty years to stop this abominable business. They challenged the exploitation of India even though, if anything, it would hurt their own social class's economic wealth.

Most of those in the Clapham group were evangelical dissenters, that is, Methodists and others who had left or were working against the establishment in the then widely corrupt Church of England. But they did not use their political skills and power to protect the position of dissenters or to force reforms onto the Church of England. They spent themselves—totally and consistently—to seek the greater good of others, not to protect themselves.

Fifth, Wilberforce and his fellow evangelicals acted thoughtfully. They only took on issues of the day after careful study and much prayer and study of the Bible. Often they would spend years gathering facts on a certain issue before publicly taking it on. One of the Clapham group, Thomas Clarkson, was a noted researcher who carefully gathered facts and formulated arguments before Wilberforce or the others would speak out publicly on an issue. For years he gathered information on the slave trade by interviewing thousands of sailors who were involved in it. William Carey—the famed missionary to India—played a key role in providing information and insights that led to the 1813 passage of reforms in British policies toward India.[5] Wilberforce and his fellow reformers acted together. They tested their ideas on each other; the insights of one would correct those of another. When they spoke—whether on policy toward India, child labor in the mines, or slavery—they had their facts straight, having carefully thought through their positions. They could defend their positions with skill and knowledge.

William Wilberforce and American Evangelicals Today

Are American evangelicals today true heirs of Wilberforce and his fellow reformers of two hundred years ago? Are we working—persistently and passionately—for reforms in our country's public policies, in spite of opposition and ridicule? Are we concerned for those suffering in our country and around the world with the same passion Wilberforce had for the slaves in his day?

Forty years ago I would have answered that question with a sad no. American Christians—and especially evangelicals—saw politics as "dirty" and something from which one should "keep oneself from being polluted by the world" (James 1:27). In 1965 Jerry Falwell, in a sermon he later rightly regretted, warned against preachers who became politically involved instead of sticking to preaching the gospel of salvation through Jesus Christ.[6]

But much has changed. Jerry Falwell became a leading voice calling for Christian political involvement. Organizations such as the Christian Coalition, Call to Renewal, the Family Research Council, Evangelicals for Social Action, Focus on the Family, the Evangelical Environmental Network, and many other voices in the political arena are calling evangelical Christians into active political involvement. Key evangelical leaders are speaking out on public-policy issues of the day.

Hundreds of thousands of evangelicals have responded. Many have joined and sent money to organizations such as those mentioned above; others have registered to vote and perhaps for the first time have cast ballots; others have passed out voters' guides at their churches or taken part in other volunteer political activities. Some have been stimulated to run for public office or to work for the election of certain candidates. This is all to the good. We have increasingly followed William Wilberforce in his concern for changing the nation's public policies.

However, there have been days when, observing my fellow evangelicals deeply involved in seeking to influence public policies, I wished they had all gone back to sitting quietly in their pews! In crucial ways we have not followed the example of Wilberforce and his fellow evangelicals. We have rushed in when we should have held back and held back when we should have rushed in. We have tackled minor evils with gusto, and ignored more serious evils. Sometimes we have acted more as a narrow, special-interest group working for advantages for ourselves rather than for others in need. At times our rhetoric has been shrill and our grasp of facts thin. We have been used by political operatives to advance their partisan interests, and then we've been ignored when actual policy decisions were made. It is all too easy to enter the political arena with distorted agendas and inept tactics.

More specifically, there are three especially dangerous traps into which we evangelicals can fall—and at times have fallen—as we work to influence our nation's public policies. I examine each of these three traps in turn.

Three Traps to Be Avoided

The Misguided Efforts Trap

It is all too easy for us, even when we are trying to act as Christians who are obedient to our Savior, to adopt positions on public-policy issues that later we see as being simply wrong. Or we have ignored major problems and spent enormous amounts of time and energy on less important issues. During the 1960s many evangelicals spoke out against Martin Luther King Jr., and opposed his calls for national action to correct the blatant segregation then practiced in many states. When in 1990 Saddam Hussein's armies attacked Kuwait without warning or provocation, some evangelicals on the left opposed the highly successful efforts of the American-led coalition to force them out and restore Kuwait's independence. In the 1980s we largely ignored the emerging AIDS crisis in Africa that is now taking hundreds of thousands of lives, while spending enormous time and energy on trying to reinstall teacher-led prayers in public schools.

All of us see imperfectly—and through lenses clouded by missing information and our own biases. How then can we avoid stumbling into the trap of misguided efforts? How can we escape taking positions on public-policy issues that we later come to regret and see as more dishonoring than honoring of the name of Christ? How can we avoid focusing on minor issues and ignoring major issues?

The first step is to recognize a basic fact: all of us tend to view contemporary issues through lenses shaped by our own personal backgrounds and the current culture. All of us live in a certain social setting in terms of family, friends, coworkers, and neighborhood. Our natural tendency is to reflect the political views dominant in our social setting. What we have experienced and the perspectives and values that surround us seem so natural and right that we fail to recognize they are blinding us to other ways of viewing the world that may be more in keeping with biblical teachings. The danger is that as we Christians enter the political world—whether as voters or in more active roles—we will end up merely reflecting our original political predispositions, now dressed up with a little "God-talk."

The apostle Paul has given us the answer for avoiding this danger. It lies in careful use of our God-given minds. To the Christians in Rome, Paul wrote, "Do not conform any longer to the pattern of this world, but be transformed by the renewing of your mind" (Rom. 12:2). And he urged the Christians in Corinth in words as relevant today as they were two thousand years ago: "Take captive every thought to make it obedient to Christ" (2 Cor. 10:5).

As we Christian citizens vote, express our opinions, and in other ways act politically, it is essential for us to do so carefully and thoughtfully. An understanding of relevant biblical principles and of the factual situation will help us determine our priorities and ensure that we are supporting policy options that are indeed honoring to our Lord. Careful thinking will help us avoid pursuing secondary issues while ignoring more important issues—or coming out on the wrong side of contentious issues.

> "For though we live in the world, we do not wage war as the world does. The weapons we fight with are not the weapons of the world. . . . We demolish arguments and every pretension that sets itself up against the knowledge of God, and we take captive every thought to make it obedient to Christ."
>
> —PAUL, APOSTLE AND MISSIONARY, IN 2 COR. 10:3–5

In addition, "renewing our minds" will enable us to defend our positions with persuasiveness and integrity, because, having fully thought them through, we can marshal needed facts. Sometimes politically involved Christians suffer derision because of the secular bias of the mainstream news media, but sometimes the problem lies with us. At times our facts have been wrong, our voices harsh, and our arguments weak. We need clear thinking on exactly why we are taking a certain position, and we need to be able to explain those reasons to others in a clear, convincing manner. Then if our positions are distorted by secular opponents—as will sometimes happen—the fault will lie with our opponents, not with ourselves, as now is too often the case.

Wilberforce and his Clapham group of fellow believers can serve as our model here. Their minds had been transformed and their thoughts made captive to Jesus Christ. As we have seen, they acted only after careful preparation marked by Bible study, prayer, and the gathering of facts. And they worked together as a group. In doing so they were spared the sort of errors that present-day evangelical Christians have too often fallen into.

The Christian-Nation Trap

Some of my fellow evangelical Christians refer to the United States as once having been—and perhaps one day again becoming—a Christian nation. I read such statements and come away puzzled. What do they mean by the United States being a Christian nation? If by this they mean that they hope and pray that more and more Americans will come to accept Jesus Christ as their Savior from sin and their Lord, and that they will seek earnestly to pattern their lives after him, I join with them fully.

But usually those who refer to the United States as being a Christian nation seem to have something quite different in mind. They begin by emphasizing the Christian aspects of our nation's heritage and foundations (while ignoring or downplaying the less-than-Christian aspects). From there they go on to reach two conclusions: (1) that it is right and proper for our nation's public policies to favor Christianity, as long as it is favoring a generalized Christianity and not any particular denomination or set of doctrines, and (2) that as we do so, God will bless our nation, and if we do not do so, the United States will go into social and political decline. To support this position, people will cite Old Testament promises of God to bless Israel if it would follow God's commands. Often Psalm 33:12 is cited: "Blessed is the nation whose God is the Lord." And 2 Chronicles 7:14: "If my people, who are called by my name, will humble themselves and pray and seek my face and turn from their wicked ways, then will I hear from heaven and will forgive their sin and will heal their land."

In the Christian-nation mind-set, the biggest motivation for Christians to become politically involved is to make sure that Christianity is recognized in the public life of our nation. Then God will bless the United States, and we as a nation will prosper. I suspect many evangelicals who have a renewed interest in public-policy issues are motivated by this Christian-nation mind-set. Often they have done so unself-consciously and without fully thinking it through. But there it is, lurking in the background and coloring their reactions to political issues and candidates.

I see this as a trap to be avoided, however, rather than a foundation for Christian political involvement. A brochure put out by an evangelical organization recently came across my desk. It proclaimed:

> With strategic partnerships in Washington, D.C., it [the organization] is able to be proactively involved in the effort to reclaim America for Christ. Whether delivering petitions; encouraging constituents to respond to critical legislation with letters, faxes, phone calls, and e-mail; fighting for qualified judicial nominees; or registering voters; the [name of the organization] aims to provide a megaphone for the collective voice of Christ's Church.

There is a problem here, is there not? How, according to this brochure, is America to be reclaimed for Christ? Not by Christians preaching the gospel, not by winning their neighbors to Christ, not by Christian husbands and wives creating homes of mutual respect and love. No, it is by political means: petitions, constituent pressures on public officials, working to affect the judicial nomination process, and voting. It is assumed that America can be led back to Christ by political means.

But this cannot be right. Whenever in history the church has tried to advance the gospel by political means, the church has been corrupted and the gospel dishonored. Think of some European countries where churches have been officially supported and given certain privileges by the government. They have almost always ended up weakened and with declining active members. Christ offers us a new life in him; he asks us to give him our hearts. It is futile to require the acceptance of Christ's offer of a new life in him; it can only be freely accepted.

Since this is the case, ought we Christians to insist that Christian symbols and references be displayed in public places, giving the impression that Christianity is being preferred over other religions or unbelief? Ought the public schools subject children from Jewish, Muslim, or unbelieving families to Christian rituals and prayers? These are complicated issues, and I will discuss them later in this book. They need to be thought through carefully and with sensitivity to our non-Christian fellow citizens. But the Christian-nation mind-set focuses on the Christian heritage of our country, sees that the strong majority of American are Christians—at least in a very broad sense of the word—and concludes we have a right to insist that a gloss of Christian symbols and references be imposed on all.

Sometimes I am invited to speak to church groups about Christianity and the political realm. I often make the point that Christianity is sometimes disadvantaged today by our government's public policies. I will say more about this in a later chapter. But I always am certain to add that I believe we Christians ought to be as concerned for the religious freedom of our Jewish or Muslim neighbors and for the rights of our nonbelieving neighbors to live out their lack of religious beliefs as we are for our own religious freedom. If we do not do this, we become like any other special-interest group, working for advantages for ourselves.

In addition, it is irresponsible for us evangelicals, who have a high view of Scripture, to apply the promises and warnings made to the Old Testament nation of Israel to the present-day United States. There is no biblical basis for believing that God has made a special covenant with the United States or named Americans as his chosen people. Today God works through his worldwide church, which is drawn out of "every nation, tribe, people and language" (Rev. 7:9), not through a special, chosen nation. The United States is not the equivalent of Old Testament Israel.

"The real issue today is not whether one is a Democrat or a Republican, but whether one is committed to justice for all. This means we must defend the rights of those with whom we disagree. Suppressing their freedoms in the name of religion is just as wrong as for them to suppress ours."[7]

—ED DOBSON, PASTOR AND FORMER OFFICIAL WITH MORAL MAJORITY

Again Wilberforce and the Clapham group can serve as a model. They certainly were concerned with spreading the gospel and worked to encourage their countrymen to live more Christlike lives. Wilberforce's book *Real Christianity*, a classic of Christian devotional literature, is still in print and can be read with benefit today.[8] In it he urged the British people of his day to take their Christian faith more seriously and to live more consistently Christian lives. But in their political activities, the

Clapham group worked for freedom and more equitable treatment for others. Their primary goal was not to protect their own religious freedom or to promote Christianity by the use of public policies. Their concern was not to make Britain into a great nation. In fact, their efforts to end the slave trade and the purely exploitive policies toward India were seen in their day as weakening Britain economically and damaging its great-nation status. Their concern was to be faithful to a God of love, who cares for all his children of whatever nationality or race.

It is easy for concerned Christian citizens who do not pause to think through their political involvement to slip into a Christian-nation mind-set. It is easy to assume that the primary motive for Christians to be concerned with public-policy issues is to make sure that Christianity is honored and even given some advantages over other religious and secular faiths. And that is wrong.

The Trap of Despair

To many of us, government and public policies appear enormously complex. And so they are. The Christian citizen wishing to act in a responsible, contributing manner is faced with a host of policy alternatives and controversies on the national, state, and local levels. It would be a full-time job to master them all and take thoughtful, biblically-based positions on them. Meanwhile, we all have our other responsibilities as parents, wage-earners, students, and church leaders, and in whatever other positions God has placed us. The temptation is to give up in despair.

One can also despair upon seeing that some Christians who have engaged in well-intended political actions have been used by politicians who were more cynical and cunning than they. In 1998 a *New York Times* reporter related how a group of twenty-five leaders of the religious right fumed that "they had been used and abused, like some cheap date." Cal Thomas, the Christian columnist and former Moral Majority official, commented, "What did they expect? They have been dealing with politicians who take as much as they can get from every interest group and give back just enough to keep them on a string so that they might stay in power. Such behavior makes 'cheap date' a perfect metaphor."[9]

Again, some are tempted to give up in despair: If politics is so corrupt, so driven by a crass search for power, seeking to be a Christian influence in public policies is futile. There's no point in being courted and flattered when Christians' votes are needed and being tossed aside when the real policy decisions are made.

We need to recognize we are surrounded by a great crowd of witnesses who demonstrate that Christians can be used by God to change a nation's public policies. Again think of William Wilberforce. In our own country I am thinking of John Witherspoon, a Presbyterian pastor, who in 1768 left his native Scotland to accept the presidency of Princeton University, helped lead the colonies' independence struggle, and signed the Declaration of Independence. I am thinking of Arthur and Lewis Tappan, two brothers and committed Christian believers, who were key leaders in the American abolitionist movement. Susan B. Anthony, well-known as a fighter for women's rights, is less well-known as a committed Christian believer. In more recent times there is former senator Mark Hatfield of Oregon who opposed both abortion and the Vietnam War as unjust. There is John Perkins, whom God called to leave a comfortable life in California to return to his native Mississippi in the 1960s to work for racial reconciliation and justice. There is former congressman Tony Hall of Ohio, who, on the basis of his deep Christian faith, worked for the United States to use its abundant agricultural resources to feed more of the world's hungry. Later he served as a United States ambassador to the United Nations. We should thank God for these heroes of faith and what he accomplished through them.

"There were just so many ways to make [Christian conservatives] happy. In addition to myriad White House events, phone calls, and meetings, they could be given passes to be in the crowd greeting the president when he arrived on Air Force One or tickets for a speech he was giving in their hometown. Little trinkets like cufflinks or pens or pads of paper were passed out like business cards. . . . Making politically active Christians personally happy meant having to worry far less about the Christian political agenda."[10]

—DAVID KUO, WHITE HOUSE AIDE UNDER GEORGE W. BUSH

Today countless Christians, serving in Congress, state legislatures, city councils, school boards, executive departments, the White House, and public-policy think-tanks, are standing firm on Christian principles and refusing to be manipulated and used for partisan advantage. I have met many of them. They surely are worthy of our prayers and encouragement.

Both these witnesses and the ordinary Christian citizens to whom they look for support and encouragement need to begin with the renewing of their minds. We Christians need to grasp key biblical principles relevant to the political world and then apply them in a thoughtful way to the public-policy issues that confront us. As we do so and as we discuss these questions with fellow believers, we will be better able to evaluate the television campaign appeals to which we are subjected, as well as the news stories we see and read. We will be able to decide what public officials and what politically active groups—whether Christian or otherwise—we should support.

And that is what this book is all about. It is intended primarily for ordinary Christian citizens, who wish to vote, express their opinions, and support public-policy alternatives in a thoughtful manner in keeping with biblical principles. It is intended for Christians who wish to be salt and light as they act as citizens of their communities and our nation.

In it I do not offer neat, simple, "Christian" answers to the host of public-policy questions our nation faces today. Instead, I seek to develop some basic Christian perspectives and principles that relate to the world of public policies and politics and then demonstrate how to apply them to key public-policy questions. My basic goal is to give help in thinking through public-policy issues in a Christian manner, not to push every reader to predetermined results. And certainly not to push the agenda of either the political left or right.

The Plan of the Book

In the next four chapters, I will explain four biblical principles or perspectives important for guiding our thinking about public-policy issues. They are, I am convinced, sure and firm, because they are directly taught in the Bible or can be directly inferred from the Bible by using our God-given minds and relying on our and other Christians' observations of the world about us.

The last seven chapters apply those Christian, biblical perspectives and principles to seven of today's public-policy issues. Even here some observations will be sure and firm, but others less so. I describe certain key alternatives but will try to avoid implying that any one of these alternatives is *the* Christian answer. In concrete situations, there is room for Christians to disagree on exactly what conclusions should flow from Christian principles. This should not be surprising. Even in our daily lives, as we seek to apply basic rules for Christian living, we are sometimes puzzled about what direction to take. Spouses may disagree over how to balance competing demands of job and family. Neighbors may disagree on how best to set up a neighborhood crime-watch program. Young people may be uncertain exactly what career to pursue.

It is the same in the political realm. The Bible is no more a recipe book for resolving twenty-first-century public-policy issues than it is a recipe book for successful marriages, neighborhood cooperation, or choosing careers. But it does contain principles highly relevant for marriages, neighborhood cooperation, and choosing careers—and for public policies. It is up to us to apply those principles in concrete situations. In doing so, there will be some disagreements; even when there is, we as followers of Jesus Christ will be far ahead of others who are unthinkingly following the political predispositions they have inherited from their social setting or striving merely for personal advantage or to amass ego-satisfying power.

It is my hope and prayer that the following eleven chapters will help Christians as they seek to understand biblical principles and perspectives relevant to the world of public-policy issues and debates and apply them in a thoughtful manner.

Questions for Reflection and Discussion

1. This chapter lists five characteristics of William Wilberforce and his fellow evangelicals that enabled them to be used by God to accomplish many needed reforms in Britain two hundred years ago. Which of these five characteristics do you see as the

most important in explaining their success? On what basis did you make your selection(s)?

2. This chapter suggests Christians can fall into the trap of misguided efforts when working to influence public policies. This consists of following the positions to which one's personal background leads; they appear so right and logical, one assumes they are supported by biblical principles. Toward what sort of positions on public-policy issues does your own personal background incline you? How certain are you that these are indeed positions supported by biblical principles?

3. Do you think of the United States as a Christian nation? In what way is it and is it not a Christian nation?

4. Do you find that demands such as those of your children, job, church, and simply helping others leaves little time or energy for becoming informed on public-policy issues and questions? If so, how do you feel about this? Does it—should it—make you feel guilty? Do you think the plan of this book may help you to place public-policy issues into a Christian perspective without having to commit more time than you have?

PART ONE

BIBLICAL PRINCIPLES

2

Creation, Sin, and Redemption

"In the Beginning God Created"

(Genesis 1:1)

FOR SEVEN YEARS MY DAUGHTER was a park ranger at Grand Canyon National Park. Every time my wife and I visited her, I was amazed at the awesome beauty of what God created in the Grand Canyon. Standing on the rim of the canyon was always a deeply moving religious experience for me. The immensity, the colors, the birds wheeling about far below, and the silence that seemed to reach up and surround me never failed to give me a profound sense of the grandeur and splendor of what God created.

But that is not the entire story. Because my daughter was a park ranger, I also learned of a darker side to the story: of tourists who would carelessly and selfishly ignore numerous warnings, get into trouble due to heat exhaustion or falls, and then have to be rescued by park rangers. And there were even darker evils present: drunken brawls and people who committed suicide by leaping from the rim of the canyon. There were drug abuse and domestic violence among some park employees. Dark, bitter evil coexisted with the most profound beauties of God's creation.

31

But neither is this the whole story. I also learned of park rangers—many of whom could command larger salaries and more prestigious positions elsewhere—who protect the beauties of the Grand Canyon from being despoiled by thoughtless visitors and protect visitors from their own foolishness and self-centeredness. I recall one particularly dramatic event. A private plane that was carelessly overloaded attempted to take off from a nearby airport, failed to gain altitude, and crashed in a heavily forested area. Park rangers hiked back to the site of the crash. They found two fatalities, but a third person, a woman, was clinging to life while trapped in the wreckage of the plane. One ranger crawled into the wreckage to administer emergency first aid. She was alive but barely. Other rangers on the scene could smell leaking fuel and saw some vapor escaping from out of the wreckage. The danger from fire and unknown toxic fumes was high. The ranger in charge ordered everyone away from the wreckage until their safety could be assured. But the ranger who had crawled into the wreckage of the plane refused to leave his patient, even at the risk of his own life. As a result, against all odds, she survived. This ranger thereby joined a long list of heroic first responders who place others before their own safety . . . and gave a poignant example of integrity and courage coexisting with death and loss.

This story illustrates much of what this chapter is about. God created a good world of almost unbelievable beauty and potential, but that creation has been profoundly marred by human sinfulness. It is a broken world that is not as it is supposed to be.[1] Yet God's grace is still at work, limiting the effects of human sinfulness and bringing hope and healing to a broken creation. In this chapter we will together examine these three themes: God's work as Creator, the invasion of sin into his perfect world, and how he is working to heal and redeem his creation.

These three themes may appear to be far removed from thinking about public policies today, and, for example, whether or not and in what ways God expects us Christians to support health-care reform or programs to oppose terrorist attacks or our government's efforts to feed starving people in Africa. Indeed, God's great acts of creation, humankind's fall into sin, and the redeeming work of Jesus Christ do not provide ready answers to today's public-policy questions. But they are like the pilings driven deep into the earth that support an eighty-story skyscraper. They are unseen, but they are vital. Without them the building would collapse.

So bear with me as we take what may appear to be a detour. The last section of this chapter will make clear how thinking about creation, sin, and redemption are crucial to right thinking about today's public-policy issues.

God's Perfect Creation

God Created a Perfect World

"In the beginning God created the heavens and the earth" (Gen. 1:1). And by his own testimony he created it "good," even very good. Six times Genesis 1 recounts that God saw what he had made and declared it good, and then at the end of his creating activities, we are told that "God saw all that he had made, and it was very good" (Gen. 1:31). Job 38–40 gives us a moving picture of God's delight in his creation. God rejoiced when "the morning stars sang together // and all the angels shouted for joy" (Job 38:7). The Grand Canyon is surely one of the features of his world in which God takes a special delight.

Human Beings' God-Given Task of Caring for His Creation

God's new-born creation was indeed very good. But that does not mean it was fully developed or had already realized its full potential. Theologian Albert Wolters has likened God's new world after the six days of creation to a baby who has been born healthy and well.[2] All parents will enthusiastically declare that their baby is good, even very good. Newborn babies are no less than miracles from the hands of God: vigorous, hearty, responsive—and resembling the father or mother or some other relative. But this does not mean newborn babies have reached their full potential. Hardly! They need to grow and develop. But what potential! With the proper growth, guidance, and support, a baby may become a skillful carpenter, a beloved pastor, a concert pianist, a caring parent, a dependable businessperson, or a thoughtful political leader.

Similarly, God's new creation was very good, but it needed development to bring out all the riches and potential God had placed in it. Even in a perfect, sinless world, God's clear intent was that through human beings' efforts the world would become populated, societies organized, cities built, music written, sculptures created, and telephones, trains, and a host of other conveniences invented. The potential for all this and more was placed—and in a sense hidden—in God's good earth. Adam and Eve and their descendants were given the task of uncovering and bringing these potentials to reality.

Genesis 1:27–28 is clear:

> God created man in his own image,
>   in the image of God he created him;
>   male and female he created them.
> God blessed them and said to them, "Be fruitful and increase in number;
> fill the earth and subdue it. Rule over the fish of the sea and the birds
> of the air and over every living creature that moves on the ground."

Two key points testify to humankind's God-given task of developing God's world and bringing to reality the potentials God placed in his creation. First, God created human beings in his image. We are image bearers of God himself, and therein lies our uniqueness. As God's image bearers, human beings are choosing, willing, creative beings. We have the capacity to discover, unfold, and develop the rich potentials God has put in his world.

This leads to and makes possible the second point present in Genesis 1:28: what has been called the cultural mandate. God explicitly gave Adam and Eve and their descendants the task of filling the earth, subduing it, and ruling over the animals God had created. This is further supported by Genesis 2:15, which relates that "the LORD God took the man and put him in the Garden of Eden to work it and take care of it." The garden of Eden was idyllic, but Adam and Eve did not simply sit around all day as though on a vacation. They had work to do—joyful, productive work, but work nonetheless. They were to take care of the garden of Eden, to improve it, to discover and develop the riches God had placed there.

The farmer who enriches the soil to make it more productive by the judicious use of fertilizers or who strengthens a strain of cattle by selective breeding practices is fulfilling God's mandate first given to Adam and Eve. So also is an athlete who hones his or her God-given skills. This is true as well of a research scientist who discovers new laws of nature present in creation and the inventor who fashions a new device that makes human life more enjoyable. One can also think of writers, producers, and actors who together put together a feature film that entertains, gives joy, instructs, and lifts the human spirit. The examples of human beings creatively using what God originally placed in his world at its creation to bring joy to the world could be multiplied indefinitely.

Shalom

The Hebrew word *shalom* is usually translated "peace," but our English word *peace* fails to capture its full meaning. Shalom refers not simply to an absence of fighting or conflict, or to a peace marked by rest and quiet. Shalom is not the peace one finds in a graveyard. Instead, it refers to a peace that grows out of harmony and right relationships. When men and women are in a right, God-intended relationship with him, each other, and the natural world, there will be order and harmony—even while there is a pulsating energy and dynamism. Think of a complex machine with many moving parts that all work together to accomplish a given task. Or imagine a basketball team that smoothly works together to win a game. In both of these examples there is activity—a pulsating, driving activity—but also shalom, because the parts are working harmoniously together in the intended manner. Shalom is the peace one finds among people who delight in living, working, and achieving together.[3]

A full and perfect shalom marked God's original creation. Adam and Eve lived in a right relationship with each other, God, and the beautiful garden where God had placed them. They worked the garden and took care of it. Shalom was fully present.

Government in a Perfect World

I make one more important point in regard to God's good creation. Even if sin had never entered the world, some form of government would have been necessary. It would be government different from those we know today: governments that must hire police and build prisons to enforce laws, which themselves are imperfect. But even in a perfect world, as Adam and Eve's descendants multiplied and filled the earth, there would have had to have been some means to create rules that would have made it possible for human societies to develop and for people in them to live together in order and harmony. There would have had to have been a way to regulate trade and commerce, probably including the creation of money, a way to decide jointly where cities should be located and to organize the different sections of the cities, and, once automobiles had been invented, something as simple as deciding on which side of the roads people should drive. Even in a sinless world, as human beings developed all the possibilities God had placed in his creation, some society-wide policies would have to have been established. This means government—even if the governments and the processes of making decisions would have looked very different from what we find in governments today.

All this has huge implications for our role today as citizens. God created his world good and perfect. And government was to be a means by which men and women would be enabled to work together to fulfill their task of unfolding and developing God's good creation. Shalom would thereby be assured. As we will see next, governments have been corrupted; they no longer are as they should be. But when Christian citizens work to bring public policies more in line with God's intent for government, they are working to call something God has created back to its original purpose. They are engaged in God's work.

The Fall

The Human Race's Rebellion against God

It is clear that something has gone terribly wrong with God's creation. From the gas chambers of Auschwitz to suicide terrorist bombers, from corporate executives who defraud their employees and stockholders to petty high-school cliques that put down those who are not part of the "in crowd," human beings give evidence of evil that is real, dark, and seemingly ever with us. As a result, shalom lies broken.

Genesis 3 reveals what has gone wrong. Adam and Eve—who had been given freedom to serve God joyfully and to work and keep the garden in which he had placed them—used that freedom to join the rebellion of Satan and his dark hosts against their Creator. The one tree whose fruit they had been told they might not eat is the tree from which they ate, because they wanted to "be like God, knowing good and evil." Moreover, the fruit was "pleasing to the eye, and also desirable for gaining wisdom" (Gen. 3:5–6). The results were immediate and catastrophic. Shalom was broken, as Adam blamed Eve and indirectly even God for having created Eve, and Eve blamed the serpent, Satan (Gen. 3:12–13).

As a result the entire human race became, as it were, addicted to sin. This ingrained habit, this compulsion, is graphically described by Jesus Christ when he walked among us: "What comes out of a man is what makes him 'unclean.' For from within, out of men's hearts, come evil thoughts, sexual immorality, theft, murder, adultery, greed, malice, deceit, lewdness, envy, slander, arrogance and folly. All these evils come from inside and make a man 'unclean' " (Mark 7:20–23). To find compelling evidence for the reality of sin, one need look no further than any television news show—or into one's own heart. This means that evil cannot be eradicated by more education, economic changes, certain political structures, or other such means by which people down through the ages have attempted to eliminate evil and re-create the perfect society.

At its core the evil that lies in all of our hearts is excessive self-love, self-gratification, and pride. Some of us as children were taught the JOY acrostic: Jesus first; others second; yourself last. Sin turns this acrostic on its head: yourself first; others and Jesus when you get around to it. Paul once described those who are living without Christ as people whose "god is their stomach" (Phil. 3:19). Their earthly desires—their self-love or self-gratification—rule their lives. In Romans 1:29 Paul lists the vile fruit of excessive self-love or pride: "envy, murder, strife, deceit and malice." There is hope, and we will explore it shortly. But

> "If only there were evil people somewhere, insidiously committing evil deeds, and it were necessary only to separate them from the rest of us and destroy them. But the line dividing good and evil cuts through the heart of every human being."[4]
>
> —ALEKSANDR SOLZHENITSYN, RUSSIAN WRITER

this hope does not come from within human beings; it comes from God himself in the form of his Son, our Savior.

Sin Destroys Shalom

Sin destroys shalom, destroys the peace and harmony that comes from people living in a right relationship with God, each other, and the natural creation. Sin places self-love ahead of God, ahead of others, and ahead of the natural creation. As a result sin is not simply a personal or private matter. It eats away at the mutual respect on which shalom and community rest. Thus sin naturally—if left unchecked—acts to alienate human beings from God and from each other and the rest of creation. Exploitation replaces cooperation; manipulation replaces mutual respect; neglect replaces a loving concern. The end result is disintegration of society and the shalom that marks society as God intended it to be. Sin corrupts all it touches: marriages, friendships, economic relationships, government and politics, art and entertainment, science and technology, and more. At the most extreme, sin leads to slavery, genocide, murder, rape, domestic violence, and racism.

Sin Corrupts All of God's Creation

Sin not only affects human relationships, it affects—one could say infects—all of God's creation. All human relationships are affected: those between husbands and wives and between parents and children, those among coworkers, races, and social classes, those among the nations of the world.

Genesis 3 clearly indicates sin also affects the natural creation. Adam is told the ground is cursed because of his sin: "Cursed is the ground because of you; // through painful toil you will eat of it // all the days of your life" (Gen. 3:17). Eve was told she would suffer pain in childbirth. The apostle Paul declares: "We know that the whole creation has been groaning in the pains of childbirth right up to the present time" (Rom. 8:22). He also refers to the creation waiting "in eager expectation for the sons of God to be revealed," and to "be liberated from its bondage to decay" (Rom. 8:19, 21). Exactly in what ways the natural creation has suffered because of humankind's sin is open to question; the fact that it has suffered and is now corrupted and distorted is not.

Redemption

God Himself Came to Earth in Human Form

Immediately after the fall into sin by Adam and Eve—after their joining Satan's rebellion against God—God in his great love and mercy did not leave our human parents to wallow in their sin and to suffer the full consequences of that sin. God came searching for Adam and Eve, even when they foolishly tried to hide from him. And he promised that one day an offspring of the woman would crush Satan (Gen. 3:15).

Thousands of years later that promise was gloriously fulfilled on a lonely Judean night, when a baby was born in a drafty, smelly stable to a Jewish virgin. God himself broke into human history to set right what had gone so terribly wrong in the garden of Eden. The birth, life, death, and resurrection of Jesus Christ are filled with paradoxes. The all-powerful Creator of the universe, God himself, was born as a helpless baby to the most ordinary of families, among a seemingly insignificant people who were being cruelly oppressed by a foreign power.

The paradoxes of Christ's work continued throughout his lifetime. The Lord of the universe went about as an itinerant rabbi, associating with the poor, sick, and outcasts of his society, and condemning the religious leaders of the day. He was finally put to death by way of a horrific beating and the most torturous death known to the Roman Empire: crucifixion. But

> "To concentrate on our rebellion, defection, and folly—to say to the world 'I have some bad news and I have some bad news'—is to forget that the center of the Christian religion is not our sin but our Savior."[5]
>
> —CORNELIUS PLANTINGA JR., PRESIDENT, CALVIN THEOLOGICAL SEMINARY

then he arose from the dead in power and might and returned to heaven, with his work accomplished. Jesus, God himself, came to our planet, made a way of salvation available to all who believe in

him, and continues to lead people to himself. Of this we can be
certain.

The Breadth and Depth of Christ's Redeeming Work

More needs to be said, however. I earlier emphasized the breadth
of the effects of human sin in corrupting and distorting all human
relationships and even the natural world, because doing so leads to
a broad view of Christ's redeeming work. Just as humankind's sin
distorted all human relationships, so also all human relationships
need to be, and can be, redeemed through Jesus Christ. As theologian Cornelius Plantinga has written: "The whole world belongs to
God, the whole world has fallen, and so the whole world needs to
be redeemed—every last person, place, organization, and program."[6]
Families, neighborhoods, friendships, places of work, economic activities, artistic endeavors, sports, entertainment, and more belong
to God, have fallen, and need to be redeemed. Why? Because God
cares about them. Why? Because they are all his. This also includes
political institutions and processes. They have been distorted by sin
and have often been turned to evil purposes. But they are still part
of the world Jesus Christ came to redeem.

"There is not a square inch in the
whole domain of our human
existence over which Christ,
who is Sovereign over *all*,
does not cry out: 'Mine!' "[7]

—ABRAHAM KUYPER (1837–1920),
DUTCH THEOLOGIAN AND STATESMAN

Sometimes Christians make
the error of seeing Christ's redeeming work as dealing only
with a narrowly conceived
spiritual realm. Under this view,
Christ's work bears on my walk
with God, is a means to the forgiveness of sins, and assures me
of life everlasting in God's house.
All this is wondrously, gloriously
true. But the full truth is even
more wondrous and more glorious. Christ came to set all human
relationships right.

Christ's Work of Redemption Is Ongoing

There is, so to speak, a battle going on that pits Christ and his
followers against Satan and his followers. There is no doubt who the

final victor will be. Christ, through his death on the cross and his resurrection, has secured the victory. One day

> at the name of Jesus every knee should bow,
>   in heaven and on earth and under the earth,
> and every tongue confess that Jesus Christ is Lord,
>   to the glory of God the Father. (Phil. 2:10–11)

Our Lord's victory over Satan and his dark forces of evil is assured, but the war goes on. There will be reverses; pain, death, and sorrow are still with us. But we know the final outcome. The trajectory was determined on Calvary and by the empty tomb.

Christians Are Agents of Christ's Redemption

In this great battle being waged, Christians are called to faithful service for their Lord. Paul refers to God "reconciling the world to himself in Christ." In that same passage he continues: "All this is from God, who reconciled us to himself through Christ *and gave us the ministry of reconciliation.* . . . We are therefore Christ's ambassadors, as though God were making his appeal through us" (2 Cor. 5:18, 20).

Since Christ's work of redemption is ongoing, and since Christians are agents of that redemption, the profound and powerful conclusion is that we are called to be God's agents of reconciliation in all aspects of life. Albert Wolters has expressed it well:

> Marriage should not be avoided by Christians, but sanctified. Emotions should not be repressed, but purified. Sexuality is not simply to be shunned, but redeemed. Politics should not be declared off-limits, but reformed. Art ought not to be pronounced worldly, but claimed for Christ. Business must no longer be relegated to the secular world, but must be made to conform again to God-honoring standards. Every sector of human life yields such examples."[8]

This truly is the glorious task to which God is calling his followers here on earth. As we are faithful to this calling, we can be used by God to be his agents of reconciliation and redemption in a fallen world. This is the truth that William Wilberforce and his evangelical allies recognized and acted upon in nineteenth-century Britain. As a result, God was able to use them as a healing force in a world that was broken, even as our world today is sadly broken.

This overview of God's good creation, its fall into sin, and its re-demption in Christ Jesus explains much of what we can observe in the world today. This world can be a place of almost unbelievable beauty and joy—of shalom in its fullest and deepest meaning. Earlier I mentioned the Grand Canyon with its grandeur, shifting colors, and quiet. Or think of two young lovers who agree to marry and are planning to establish a home based on love and mutual respect. Or a gardener who tends his tomatoes all summer so he can share them with the neighborhood when August arrives.

But this is also a world of pain and death—of 9/11, of hurricanes that kill hundreds, of people who use the disorder that comes with natural disasters to loot and pillage, of cancer that strikes unexpect-edly, of terrorists who behead their victims in front of video cameras, and of young men and women in the military who die thousands of miles away from home and family.

Yet there is more. There is good news as well as bad news. There is a neighborhood that rallies with offers of help and support when it learns of a family that has lost its house due to a fire. Billions of dollars are freely donated after a major natural disaster. First respond-ers rush into swollen streams or burning buildings to rescue those in danger.

In his famous Chronicles of Narnia series of stories for children, C. S. Lewis at various points refers to Aslan—the great lion who is a Christ figure—as being "on the move." In our world today Jesus Christ is on the move. He is real; he is present. His redeeming, reconciling, healing work is progressing. But he has also not yet come in his full power and glory. That lies in the future. Until that day Christians are called to be Christ's instruments for reconciliation and healing in a broken world.

So What?

Here—as at the end of each of the four chapters that develop basic principles—I answer the "so what?" question. I will seek to dem-onstrate that what to some may appear to be abstract principles, far removed from the hurly-burly of contemporary public-policy debates, are in fact highly relevant. Without them we would start out on the wrong road, one that will not bring us home.

Three insights especially helpful in weighing public-policy issues emerge from the perspectives on creation, sin, and redemption presented in this chapter. The first is that *it is essential for Christian citizens to care about public policies and to influence the direction they take.* Some Christians believe that governments and the public policies they enact are inherently or necessarily wrong or evil. But some sort of government would have been necessary even if sin had never entered God's good creation. Sometimes it seems the political world attracts more than its share of people who are driven by selfish pride and a push toward self-aggrandizement. But, as we have seen in this chapter, all of God's creation was created "very good," all has been corrupted by sin, and all has also been redeemed by Christ. And we are his agents of redemption; we are to work to put right what sin has corrupted. This includes the political realm. The evils that often are all too evident in the political world may in part be due to Christians failing to be the salt and light they are called to be in that world.

A second key insight that arises from this chapter is that *sin is real and present in a fallen world, including in the political world itself.* Thus we should be on guard against the perversion of government toward evil ends. And we should expect that even when gains by way of public policies come, they will come only after great struggle and be of a limited nature. Christians must avoid a triumphalism that believes society will be perfected or that God's kingdom on earth will come by way of the public policies they by their own efforts enact. It is because of the continuing presence and power of sin that the Christian-nation idea discussed in chapter 1 fails. Neither the United States nor any other nation is going to be claimed for Christ by political means. The corruptions of sin are too much everywhere around us—and within us.

As I wrote in chapter 1, God uses Christians now, as he has in the past, to make a genuine difference in public policies. Christ has come, and he is reclaiming his creation. But this is different from saying that public-policy success will always come, or that it will come easily. Usually success will come slowly and only to a limited extent. Sometimes it will not come at all. Sometimes government itself—instead of being an instrument of reconciliation—will be perverted to serve evil ends.

This means that Christian citizens should not buy into utopian promises of what public policies can deliver. These dreams are founded on false beliefs that the evil we see all around us in this world is found not within all of our hearts, but in certain social or economic conditions or in certain especially evil people. If one believes this, then changing social or economic conditions or getting rid of especially evil people will usher in a world of peace, joy, and opportunity for all.

But Christians know that raising education standards, changing economic conditions, or eliminating racism is not going to lead to the perfect society or even a great society. Nor is shalom going to result from removing an Adolf Hitler, a Saddam Hussein, or an Osama bin Laden. After the fall of communism in 1989, we quickly learned that this did not mean the world was going to be a peaceful place with no more threats and dangers. One tyranny was quickly replaced by other tyrannies and threats. And so it will always be until our Lord returns in great power and every knee bows before Jesus Christ and every tongue confesses that he is Lord.

This is not a council of despair. Far from it! But the continuing presence and power of sin in our broken world means we should not expect that government and public policies will usher in a society or a world of perfect shalom. That day awaits the return of our Lord.

A third insight flows from our consideration of creation, sin, and redemption: that *public policies can be changed for the better by dedicated Christians and doing so can make a meaningful difference.* While guarding against an easy optimism concerning what governments and public policies can accomplish—as I just stressed—we must also guard against a deep pessimism that says governments are always the same and we as Christian citizens cannot change public policies for the good. Christ is on the move; the Holy Spirit has been poured out on his church; Satan has been defeated. Therefore, there is reason to believe that Christians' efforts at healing a broken world will often meet with some success.

In chapter 1 we met William Wilberforce and the evangelical Clapham group that achieved much good in nineteenth-century Britain. We more briefly met other dedicated Christians who were not subverted by the political process and whom God as a result was able to use to achieve much good in our country.

I could fill volumes recounting stories of dedicated, committed Christian believers who, acting on the basis of their faith in Jesus Christ, have been used by God to change public policies—changes that went on to touch many persons for good. They acted as instruments of God's healing in a hurting, broken world. They served as his agents of reconciliation and redemption in a world that is being redeemed by Christ but is still not yet as it is supposed to be.

Questions for Reflection and Discussion

1. The chapter begins with an illustration of the Grand Canyon as a place of great beauty and goodness, selfishness and evil, and integrity all existing together. Give other examples from your own experience or from events reported in the news where these exist together in one place.

2. Try to imagine how the world and the human race would have developed if sin had never entered the world. Would we be living in houses as we do today? Would there be cities as we know them? What about cars, TVs, video games, Blackberries, and computers? What do you think governments would be like?

3. The chapter argues that Christians are called to be God's agents of reconciliation and redemption. What does this mean for our personal and family lives? Then consider what this means for fields such as entertainment, sports, business, and politics.

4. The chapter argues we should work to keep a balance between expecting too much from public policies (as though they will lead to a near-perfect society) and expecting too little (as though public policies never will make a real difference). Do you tend to expect too much or too little from governments and the public policies they enact? Or do you tend to strike a healthy balance?

3

Justice

"Follow Justice and Justice Alone"

(Deuteronomy 16:20)

ON FEBRUARY 2, 2006, AT THE NATIONAL PRAYER BREAKFAST in Washington, D.C., some three thousand people packed a hotel ballroom. President George W. Bush, King Abdullah of Jordan, a host of ambassadors and other foreign dignitaries, scores of senators and congressmen, and many nationally known church leaders were all in attendance. But the main speaker was not one of the famous church leaders or politicians, as is usually the case at these annual gatherings. Instead, it was a famous entertainer: the Irish singer Bono of the band U2. He spoke eloquently of justice:

> This is not about charity in the end, is it? It's about justice. . . . And that's too bad. Because we're good at charity. Americans, Irish people, are good at charity. We like to give, and we give a lot, even those who can't afford it. But justice is a higher standard. . . .
> Preventing the poorest of the poor from selling their products while we sing the virtues of the free market, that's not charity: That's a justice issue. Holding children to ransom for the debts of their grandparents, that's not charity: That's a justice issue. Withholding life-saving medicines out of deference to the Office of Patents, well that's not charity. To me, that's a justice issue.[1]

The world of governments and public policy debates is a tough, contentious, confusing world. It is far removed from our everyday lives of work, family, shopping, soccer leagues, church, and friends. Most of us will never hold public office. How are we as Christian citizens—acting as Christ's agents of redemption in the political realm—to know what public policies to support and what to oppose? How are we to be salt and light in the public-policy realm? There is no single, simple answer to that question. The place to start, however, is where Bono started: thinking about justice as God's intention for governments.

But exactly what is the justice of which Bono spoke? He gave examples of it, but he never really said what it is. Justice is one of those ideals that all of us are for, but few of us can explain what exactly it is. What does it mean for us in twenty-first-century America? How are we to recognize it when we see it? The Bible speaks repeatedly of justice, as in the subtitle of this chapter taken from Deuteronomy 16. But how can we explain in plain words why justice plays such a big role in the Bible?

These are crucial questions for which we need to search the Scriptures for answers. As we will soon see, justice lies at the heart of what God intends governments and their public policies to be all about. Therefore, Christians' evaluations of public policies should also be about justice. As we more fully understand the biblical standard of justice, we will be putting in place a second key element that will enable us to think as Christians about the often puzzling world of public policies.

In this chapter I first briefly consider government as a God-established institution. Next I consider the biblical understanding of justice. The final section of the chapter applies all this to the real-world of public policies by answering the "so what?" question.

Government as Part of God's Provision

Governments and the public policies they enact are a part of God's gracious provision for his world. The Bible teaches God has instituted three basic human institutions: marriage and the family, the church, and government. All three are a part of his divine plan for human society. Christians usually recognize the first two of these

institutions—the family and the church—as being God instituted.
But the Bible makes clear that God has also instituted the state or
the government. Proverbs 8:15–16 declares:

> By me kings reign
>   and rulers make laws that are just;
> by me princes govern,
>   and all nobles who rule on earth.

Paul wrote in Romans 13, "there is no [governing] authority except
that which God has established" and then he refers to governing
authorities as "what God has instituted" and as "God's servant" (Rom.
13:1, 2, 4). When Jesus was before Pilate and refused to answer
some of his questions, Pilate in exasperation asked, "Do you refuse
to speak to me?" And, "Don't you realize I have power to free you
or to crucify you?" Jesus responded, "You would have no power over
me if it were not given to you from above" (John 19:10–11). The
Bible clearly testifies that the authority of governing officials comes
from God.

Of course, human governments are by their very nature fallen
governments, prone to sinful, selfish actions. As we saw in the previous chapter, sin has infected all of God's creation. But Christ has also
overcome sin and is working to redeem all of his creation—including
the political world of presidents, legislatures, judges, laws, and public
policies.

Justice

Bono was on the right track when he challenged the powerful leaders
at the prayer breakfast to pursue justice. When the Israelites—after
wandering in the desert for forty years—were ready to enter the land
God had promised them, God gave these instructions to Moses: "Ap-
point judges and officials for each of your tribes in every town the
LORD your God is giving you, and they shall judge the people fairly.
Do not pervert justice or show partiality. Do not accept a bribe, for a
bribe blinds the eyes of the wise and twists the words of the righteous.
Follow justice and justice alone, so that you may live and possess the
land the LORD your God is giving you" (Deut. 16:18–20).

God has instituted governing authorities and their public policies to work against evil and to promote justice in society. This is made clear throughout the Scriptures. The Old Testament prophets repeatedly condemned the kings and other rulers of Israel for their failures to uphold a just legal system. The prophet Amos, for example, condemned those who "oppress the righteous and take bribes // and . . . deprive the poor of justice in the courts" (Amos 5:12). Psalm 72 gives a moving picture of the king—or other ruler—as God intends for those in authority to rule:

> For he will deliver the needy who cry out,
> the afflicted who have no one to help.
> He will take pity on the weak and the needy
> and save the needy from death.
> He will rescue them from oppression and violence,
> for precious is their blood in his sight. (Ps. 72:12–14)

Clearly God intended the rulers of Israel to execute justice, to avoid corruption, and to protect the poor and weak in society from exploitation by the evil and the powerful.

The New Testament testifies that this Old Testament role of government has a broader application than that of the ancient Israelites. Romans 13 is particularly clear on this point. Paul tells the church in Rome not only that rulers receive their authority from God, but also that their authority should be used to promote good and restrain evil: "For rulers hold no terror for those who do right, but for those who do wrong. Do you want to be free from fear of the one in authority? Then do what is right and he will commend you. For he is God's servant to do you good. . . . He is God's servant, an agent of wrath to bring punishment on the wrongdoer" (Rom. 13:3–4). Similarly Peter refers to "governors, who are sent by him to punish those who do wrong and to commend those who do right" (1 Peter 2:14).

This means that those who rule justly are acting as God's servants. Their calling is holy; they are doing God's redeeming work on earth. This means that judges, legislators, chief executives, civil servants, and a host of other government officials are all following a divine calling. They are God's servants in the political realm.

But What Is Justice?

If God intends rulers to rule with justice, what can we say about the nature of the justice they are to pursue? If the establishment of a more just order in society is what God intends for governments and public policies, how can we as Christian citizens determine what public policies are just and what are unjust?

Justice has traditionally been defined as giving all persons their due. There is much content in that very simple definition. It assumes that as image bearers of God himself, human beings have certain things that are due them. One can think immediately of things such as the right to life itself, the freedom to worship God as one chooses, and the opportunity to pursue a livelihood free from oppressive laws or social and economic conditions that thwart one's efforts. God intends for all human beings to be able to contribute to society and to live with creative purpose and love. Laws that enable and encourage people to live such lives are just laws. They help make possible lives marked by peace, freedom, and opportunities for creative service to God and others.

This much is a good start. But fully understanding the meaning of justice in today's world is a challenge. It is easy to become bogged down in abstract notions and hair-splitting distinctions. Turning to the Bible and using concrete examples from it will help us avoid the swamp of intangible concepts that are miles away from the real world in which we live. As already seen, the Bible is filled with references to justice and injustice. Laws and courts loom large in the Bible—usually in a context of where injustices in ancient Israel were condemned or warned against.

"Biblical justice recognizes that both punishment and meeting social needs are essential to a just society. The Bible calls for punishment—which C. S. Lewis called 'balancing the scales of justice'—not necessarily because it is a deterrent, but because justice demands it. But Scripture also demands social justice: Ancient Israelites were told to leave gleanings at the side of the field for the poor, maintain honest scales, feed the hungry, and clothe the naked."[2]

—CHARLES COLSON, FOUNDER OF PRISON FELLOWSHIP MINISTRIES

These injustices largely fall into three categories. They can serve as our guide to greater insight into the meaning of justice.

Justice and Injustice in the Bible

The first type of injustice the Bible condemns is *illegal, evil acts of immoral individuals*. God condemns criminal acts and the failure of laws and courts to protect the people from such acts. The prophet Isaiah condemns Jerusalem with these words:

> See how the faithful city
>   has become a harlot!
> She once was full of justice;
>   righteousness used to dwell in her—
>   but now murderers!
> Your silver has become dross,
>   your choice wine is diluted with water. (Isa. 1:21–22)

Here the injustice Isaiah condemned was due to the actions of immoral individuals. Murderers were living in Jerusalem with apparently no action being taken against them. Those whose lives had been taken and their families had suffered an enormous injustice. Also unjust—even if on a less severe level—were merchants who watered down the wine or mixed base materials into the silver they were selling. In effect, merchants were stealing from their customers by portraying what they were selling for something it was not. And no authorities had put a stop to such deceptions.

Thus, one form of justice governments ought to pursue is the protection of all from the illegal, criminal acts of others. That is why we speak of the criminal *justice* system. The system of laws, police, prosecutors, courts, and prisons are all designed to promote justice by prohibiting criminal acts, arresting those who violate criminal laws, bringing them to trial, and enforcing punishment upon them. In Romans, Paul explicitly refers to this justice-promoting role of government officials in these words: "He is God's servant, an agent of wrath to bring punishment on the wrongdoer" (Rom. 13:4).

The Bible condemns a second category of injustice: *governments that themselves rob people of what is due them through their oppressive acts*. The prophet Isaiah railed against the government of his day as corrupt and oppressive:

> Woe to those who make unjust laws,
>   to those who issue oppressive decrees,

> to deprive the poor of their rights
> > and withhold justice from the oppressed of my people,
> making widows their prey
> > and robbing the fatherless. (Isa.10:1–2)

Similarly the prophet Amos condemned unjust, oppressive courts:

> You oppress the righteous and take bribes
> > and you deprive the poor of justice in the courts. . . .
> Hate evil, love good;
> > maintain justice in the courts. (Amos 5:12, 15)

In Revelation 13:5–7 John's vision gives us a powerful picture of a government that has become evil and oppressive: "The beast was given a mouth to utter proud words and blasphemies and to exercise his authority for forty-two months. He opened his mouth to blaspheme God, and to slander his name and his dwelling place and those who live in heaven. He was given power to make war against the saints and to conquer them." This beast has traditionally been interpreted to symbolize Rome and its persecution of Christians under emperors such as Domitian and Nero. The martyrs' blood flowed freely in Roman theaters and coliseums. In a sinful world, government—which has been instituted by God to restrain evil and promote justice—can be turned to evil purposes and can itself become an instrument for injustice.

The communist regimes in the old Soviet Union and Eastern Europe imposed a totalitarian order that controlled their citizens' occupations, restricted their travel, denied their freedom of religion, interfered with the upbringing of their children, denied them the freedom to speak or publish their beliefs, and in numerous other ways controlled their lives. In doing so they clearly violated justice. There is then no opportunity for people to be the freely choosing, creative, morally responsible people God intends for all of us to be.

But governments can also violate justice in other, less drastic ways. A government that imposes overly burdensome taxes on one segment of its population and almost none on another, that favors secular ideologies over religious faith, that responds only to lavish campaign contributions, or that provides better schools for some neighborhoods than for others is itself acting unjustly. The government is then putting some of its citizens at certain disadvantages that make it more difficult for them to realize the opportunities that are due all people.

A third type of injustice the Bible denounces consists of *social or economic conditions present in society that unjustly limit people in their actual opportunities to live lives of freedom and responsible action.* And in the face of those unjust conditions, government—the very body God has instituted to limit the effects of sin—does nothing. Again, the Bible clearly speaks against this injustice.

Surprisingly Isaiah once railed against the very sacrifices, assemblies, and prayers that God in the Mosaic law had required:

> "The multitude of your sacrifices—
>   what are they to me?" says the LORD.
> "I have more than enough of burnt offerings,
>   of rams and the fat of fattened animals;
> I have no pleasure
>   in the blood of bulls and lambs and goats.
> When you come to appear before me,
>   who has asked this of you,
>   this trampling of my courts? . . .
> When you spread out your hands in prayer,
>   I will hide my eyes from you;
> even if you offer many prayers,
>   I will not listen." (Isa. 1:11–12, 15)

Why was God rejecting the offerings and prayers he elsewhere asked the ancient Israelites to bring to him? Isaiah gives the answer in the following words of God:

> Your hands are full of blood;
>   wash and make yourselves clean.
> Take your evil deeds
>   out of my sight!
> Stop doing wrong,
>   learn to do right!
> Seek justice,
>   encourage the oppressed.
> Defend the cause of the fatherless,
>   plead the cause of the widow. . . .
> Your rulers are rebels,
>   companions of thieves;
> they all love bribes
>   and chase after gifts.

They do not defend the cause of the fatherless;
the widow's case does not come before them. (Isa. 1:15–
17, 23)

Oppression and injustice were filling the land, and the governing rulers were doing nothing about it. Instead, they were "companions of thieves," and bribes had turned them away from pursuing justice for those in need.

Today also injustice can result from the inaction of rulers while people's ability to live in freedom and to care for their families and others is thwarted. Think of certain businesses that are allowed to pollute the environment with dangerous chemicals to the point that people are dying of cancer. Or think of members of a minority racial group who are subjected to an unrelenting prejudice that prevents them from finding meaningful, productive employment that would allow them to support their families and contribute to society as God intends them to do. Governments that fail to correct injustices such as these are themselves unjust.

Once, as a state senator in Michigan, I was contacted by a Christian, African-American mother who was working to raise two teenage daughters alone. She lived in an area of the city where prostitution was rife, and the police were doing little to curb it. She reported that it was impossible for her and her daughters to sit out on their front porch on a summer evening, or even to walk to church on a Sunday morning, without men driving by in their cars, calling out, and making lewd comments. When government—in this case the city police—fails to act in a situation such as this, it is acting unjustly. It is failing in its duty to maintain a just order. By its inaction it becomes a "co-conspirator" in the unjust conditions. In such a situation government's inaction makes it more difficult for people to live with the creative purpose and meaning that a loving God intends for them and that they may fervently desire.

As we saw earlier, an overly strong, intrusive government can itself become a source of injustice, but an overly weak government that is inactive in the face of injustices is also failing in its God-given duty to maintain justice.

Think back to William Wilberforce and his evangelical allies whom we met in chapter 1. The injustices they fought against were for the most part of this third type. It was not that the British government itself engaged in the slave trade or that it employed children as young as eight or nine to work in mines under dangerous conditions. Even the exploitive practices toward India were being carried out not directly by the government, but by the East India Company. Wilberforce took on injustices that economic and social forces in Britain were condoning and profiting from. The British government was acting in a deeply unjust manner not because of what it was doing, but because of what it was failing to do. It looked the other way as enormous injustices were inflicted on people powerless to do anything about them.

So What?

How does justice relate to today's world of public policies and to our own questions and doubts as we work to be faithful citizens? Is all this about government as God's instrument to bring about a more just order mere theory, perhaps all right for professors of political science or theology, but with no real, practical meaning for us who wish to be responsible, Christian citizens?

I am fully convinced the idea of governments being God's instruments for achieving greater justice in society is extremely practical. Its useful applications are immediate, down-to-earth, and far ranging. Yet right here many Christians stumble. Thus, it is crucial to look at three implications, or consequences, of the idea of governments pursuing justice.

Justice and the Common Good

Justice and another Christian concept, the common good, are firmly linked. Working for more justice in society will result in the advancement of the common good. The common good is that which is good for our communities and our society as a whole. The common good puts the well-being of society as a whole ahead of the well-being of certain narrow segments of society, such as certain regions of the country; certain ethnic, racial, or religious groups; or certain economic interests. When, in pursuit of justice, *all* individuals are given their due, the common good moves forward.

This speaks directly to what ought to be the motive of Christian citizens as we think about public-policy issues of the day. It certainly is right and proper for us to be concerned for justice for ourselves or for the religious or occupational groups of which we are members. But if our concern for more justice stops here, we are really not concerned about justice at all; we are acting much like any other special-interest group pushing its interests over that of the common good.

Remember William Wilberforce and his fellow evangelicals. The public-policy issues they tackled were those in which they saw the greatest injustices being perpetrated, not those in which they saw injustices that most directly affected them or their fellow evangelicals. As a result they ended up expending themselves—day-in and day-out, year-in and year-out—seeking more just public policies for people far removed from themselves and their social class. They thereby left us a powerful model of what the Christian pursuit of justice and the common good is all about.

As we begin to think about public-policy issues, our first question ought to ferret out major injustices in our nation and world today, not injustices we as American Christians may be experiencing. Sometimes the two may be the same; more often they will not. But in either case we ought to be guided by a passionate desire to correct major injustices, not to improve our own position. In so doing we are seeking the common good, not our own well-being. That is the goal of a just order; that should be the goal of Christian attempts to influence public policy.

Justice Is Inclusive

In 2003 the evangelical governor of Alabama, Bob Riley, concluded that, based on biblical principles, the Alabama tax system was unjust. Lower-income people were paying a much higher percentage of their meager incomes in taxes than were the wealthy. And the tax system was not taking in enough money to provide a quality education to children in all areas of the state. Governor Riley declared, "According to our Christian ethics, we're supposed to love God, love each other and help take care of the poor. It is immoral to charge somebody making $5,000 an income tax."[3] He persuaded the legislature to put to a vote of the people amendments to the Alabama Constitution that would revamp the structure of taxes in Alabama and provide more money for education and other services. The proposed amendments were defeated at the polls. Nevertheless, the reform proposal received national attention in the news media when Governor Riley and Susan Pace Hamill, a law professor who had also attended an evangelical seminary and was advising the governor, argued for the proposal based on the biblical principle of justice.

Whatever the merits—or lack of merits—in the arguments Riley and Hamill made in this specific instance, they were right in insisting that taxes and who pays them are questions to which the Bible and its concept of justice speaks.

Some people assume that Christianity speaks only to what are sometimes called moral issues, such as abortion, prostitution, pornography, and same-sex marriage. But this is wrong. When we focus on justice for all, we will see that it indeed speaks to such issues, but it also speaks

> "Alabamians practicing Christianity are demanding that Alabama's taxes meet the moral standards of justice required by their faith. . . . More and more Alabamians are recognizing that taxes are a moral issue that must exemplify Judeo-Christian values as revealed in the Bible."[4]
>
> —SUSAN PACE HAMILL,
> PROFESSOR OF LAW, THE UNIVERSITY
> OF ALABAMA SCHOOL OF LAW

to issues such as education, taxes, business regulation, and protection of the natural environment. Justice is an inclusive concept. Health care and educational opportunities can be distributed in an unjust manner that slants them toward the wealthy, or they can be distributed justly, with equal opportunities for all, rich and poor alike. As in the days of the Old Testament prophets, calls for greater justice must address the needs of the poor, the fatherless, and the widows who are the victims of an unjust order.

However, it is not always the poor who are victims of unjust policies. At times demagogic politicians can so inflame the public against business interests or the wealthy that tax structures or certain environmental regulations can become unjust, making it almost impossible for the honest business to succeed and prosper or for the wealthy to use the wealth they have gained by their hard work. These too are matters of justice.

The goal of "justice for all" assures that all people are afforded the freedoms and opportunities needed to develop their God-given abilities and to become what God intends for them. Thus the public policies governments pursue in *all* policy areas can be just or unjust. Injustice emerges when public policies grant or protect opportunities only for certain segments of society and ignore or stifle the freedoms and opportunities others need to be the joyful, choosing, creative people God intends them to be.

Justice Means Greater, not Less, Freedom

Some people see Christians involved in public policies as kill-joys imposing their dour view of the world and of life onto all of society. Words such as *Puritan* and *Victorian* are quickly hurled in our faces. But in fact a Christian, justice-promoting vision of public policies is freeing and liberating. Justice is a freedom-producing idea, not one that stifles and limits. People are freed to develop their gifts, to follow their passions, and to live life to the full as the responsible, loving beings God created us to be.

God has indeed made us for freedom. At the dawn of human history, in the garden of Eden, God could have made Adam and Eve without free choice; he could have made them such that they could not choose to eat from the forbidden Tree of Good and Evil. If he had done so, we would not have sinned, but we would have been less than God's image bearers. Those who love God and their neighbors because they have no choice but to do so have not really loved at all. Love

"Too many Christians today apparently feel a need for government to reflect their values in order for them to feel significant. . . . Why do so many American Christians need to feel wanted and appreciated and see their politicians reflecting the way they pray and behave? . . . Is it because of some deep sense of inferiority? Is their faith so fragile that it is only in seeing it manifested in the corridors of political power in Washington that they feel justified?"[5]

—CAL THOMAS, COLUMNIST AND FORMER OFFICIAL WITH MORAL MAJORITY

and obedience—if they are truly to be love and obedience—must be freely given. When public policies work to create a just order, they make possible—but do not force—creative, joyful, loving lives of service to others.

Sometimes Christians make the error of thinking that we should use public policies to try to force onto society whatever is good or right. Unless what is good or right also promotes greater justice in society and thereby the common good, doing so is wrong. I am fully convinced the Bible teaches homosexual relations are wrong—as are heterosexual relations outside of marriage. But does this mean either ought to be made illegal? I think not.

There is a risk here. Justice and its resulting freedoms mean there will be cheap, degrading films as well as uplifting, inspiring films, vulgar art as well as beautiful art, nudist camps as well as Bible camps, societies for the promotion of atheism as well as societies for the promotion of overseas relief and development. Some people will use the freedom and opportunities that flow from justice to make self-centered, self-aggrandizing choices. But those are their choices, and one day they will answer to God for them.

We ought to work for more justice, not to use public policies to impose our Christian beliefs or morality onto all people or to put Christianity into a favored position. That is the Christian-nation approach to public-policy issues. In chapter 1 we saw its shortcomings: Trying to use the force of law to make our nation and its people more Christian. Truly our Lord "wants all men to be saved and to come to a knowledge of the truth" (1 Tim. 2:4). But from Adam and Eve onward, he would have them come to him willingly, of their own free choice, when drawn by his love.

The goal of just public policies is to make certain that neither government itself nor other people or forces in society are discouraging or making it more difficult—or even impossible—for individuals to come to know him and to live obediently in fulfillment of his desires for all his image bearers. As I will argue later in this book, sometimes present-day public policies do exactly this, as when our public schools and state universities put forward and favor a thoroughly secular, humanistic view of the world, life, and values. But that is saying something entirely different from saying that we should strive to turn the tables and work for our public schools and state universities to put forward and favor Christian views.

One final note: There is a danger of my being misunderstood here. Often Christian ethical standards lead to justice in society. Then it is proper—and even necessary—for public policies to reflect them.

Murder, stealing, and defrauding others, for example, are all violations of the Bible's moral standards; they also all violate the standard
of justice. One can add to the list prostitution, which degrades and
exploits women caught up in this sordid business, as well as abortion, which ends a human life God has created. Therefore just public
policies will seek to outlaw and repress them. But it is their unjust
nature—their limiting and oppression of others—that makes them
proper targets of public policies, not the fact that they violate God's
moral law.

Conclusion

What I have outlined in this chapter, including in the "so what?" section, does not lead to neat, automatic answers to the public-policy
questions we face as citizens. On some questions the standards of
justice and the common good will enable us as Christians to reach
agreement. At other times they will not. However, even when there
are questions on which we reach opposite conclusions, our discus-
sions—even our debates—will be on a much higher level than if we
were not seeking answers on the basis of justice and the common
good. We will no longer be working to enrich ourselves financially or
to protect our own freedoms while forgetting those of others. Nor
will we insist on advantages for our own city or region at the expense
of other cities and regions. Nor will we be guided solely by what is
best for our own country, forgetting other nations and their peoples.
Instead we will seek justice for all. That is no small achievement.

Questions for Reflection and Discussion

1. Governments have been instituted by God for our good, but
   they often seem to fall far short of what God intends for them.
   Why do you think this is the case?

2. Justice has been traditionally defined as giving all persons their
   due. Keeping in mind what God intends for us to be as his image
   bearers, make a list of the most important things (conditions,

circumstances, or opportunities) that you believe are due all persons.

3. The chapter says there are three types of injustices that the Bible condemns or warns against. What are the three? Which one of these types of injustices do you think the United States today is most in danger of?

4. In the "so what?" section, the chapter says that public policies based on justice promote the common good, are inclusive, and lead to more freedom. Give examples of public policies that would promote the common good, be inclusive, and lead to more freedom. Then give examples of public policies that would promote the opposite: that would promote special interests of Christians, be focused on so-called specifically "moral issues," and lead to less freedom.

4

Solidarity

"Love Your Neighbor as Yourself"

(M a t t h e w   2 2 : 3 9)

IN 1940 DIET EMAN WAS A TWENTY-YEAR-OLD WOMAN living in the Netherlands. She was engaged to be married to Hein Sietsma. The two lovers were strong Christian believers and looked forward to uniting their lives together and establishing a Christ-centered home. Their future looked bright. But then on the morning of May 10, the Nazi armies attacked the Netherlands without warning and in five days overwhelmed the armed forces of that small country. A dark night of repression and horror settled over the land. Dutch Jews were particularly in danger.

When a Jewish coworker came to Diet asking for shelter, she did not hesitate. Hein was from a rural area, so she was able to arrange for the coworker and his family to live secretly with a Christian farm family. Soon both Diet and Hein became more and more involved in underground activities. They and others in their circle—all of them Christian believers—arranged for dozens of Jewish families to hide with Christian farm families and obtained forged ration cards so there would be food for them to eat. Every one of the families they hid survived the war.

At one point Diet was arrested and sent to a concentration camp, but she was later released and survived the war. However, toward the end of the war Hein was arrested by the Gestapo. He died in January 1945, in the Dachau concentration camp in Germany. Diet never saw him again. As Hein was being shipped out of the Netherlands, he managed to write a note to Diet on some bathroom tissue and threw it out of the train window. In a miracle of God's grace, some- one found it alongside the railroad tracks, located Diet, and sent her the note. In it Hein wrote: "Darling, don't count on our seeing each other again soon. . . . And here we see again that we do not decide our own lives. *Dienike* [his pet name for Diet], even if we won't see each other again on earth, we will never be sorry for what we did, that we took this stand. And know, Diet, that of every last human being in the world, I loved you the most."[1]

One can write down the names of Diet Eman and Hein Sietsma as twentieth-century heroes of faith. In the name of Jesus Christ, they loved their neighbors as themselves, even when it meant sur- rendering safety, happiness, and life itself to offer help to neighbors in desperate need. They rightly saw that they and their fellow Dutch citizens who were Jews were bound together in a common, God- created humanity. This common humanity demanded that in the face of dire conditions they give their fellow human beings des- perately needed assistance, even at the risk of their own lives.

This is the Christian principle of solidarity: the conviction that Christians cannot simply sit idly by when their fellow human be- ings are suffering and in need. It insists that we as Christians are not disconnected, isolated individuals who live our own lives without a care for others and their needs. No, as with Diet and Hein, we are called to live in solidarity with others, helping, cooperating, and supporting.

> "Please teach us Christians now to be true Christians and to put into practice what we confess, especially to these Jews. O Lord, make an end to all this, only you can do it. We know that you give strength according to our cross, but it is getting to be so very heavy, Lord."[2]
>
> —DIET EMAN, FROM A PRAYER IN HER WARTIME DIARY

This chapter considers this principle of solidarity. I first consider more fully what solidarity is, as well as its biblical basis. I next con-

sider some boundaries or limits to the application of the principle.
In the last section I consider several key implications that solidarity
has for a Christian approach to public-policy issues and questions.
It is not an abstract, theoretical principle, but is as relevant to our
lives today as this morning's headlines.

Solidarity and Its Biblical Basis

The principle of solidarity insists that we all share responsibility for
the well-being of others. When our Lord tells us that our whole duty is
summed up in the command to love God above all and our neighbors
as ourselves (Matt. 22:37–40), he teaches us that all people have a
mutual obligation to love one another. God's Word speaks clearly to
this. The apostle Paul instructs us to "let no debt remain outstand-
ing, except the continuing debt to love one another" (Rom. 13:8).
As Christians we have, as it were, a debt we owe our fellow human
beings. We owe them love. This is an obligation, a responsibility, as
real as the money we owe the bank that finances the mortgage on our
house. God has placed this obligation on us. And love means showing
concern for and offering help to others. This is solidarity.

Diet and Hein recognized and accepted the fact that as Christians
they owed what help they could give to the Jews of their country—
who were being subjected to horrors beyond imagination by their
Nazi oppressors—even though doing so put Diet and Hein's own
safety and lives at risk. They were convinced that to do otherwise
would be to fail to love one's neighbor as one's self.

The parable of the Good Samaritan has much to teach us about
solidarity. The Samaritan was truly good because he offered help
to a fellow human being in need, even though the victim was an
unknown Jew. And Jews despised Samaritans. Yet the Good Samaritan recognized a solidarity with the hurt and bleeding Jew. He offered all the help he could give. It is this obligation or responsibility
toward others—rooted in the command to love our neighbors as
ourselves—that solidarity is all about. It is a network of obligations
that bind us to all of humanity in a web of mutual love, concern,
and help.

Solidarity encompasses individuals of different races, religions, and
geographic locations, as well as those who live close to us and are

similar to us. Experience teaches us it is a lot easier for most of us to show solidarity with people who are close to us in terms of family, region, nationality, race, ethnicity, social status, and education. We identify more easily with people who are like us than those who are dissimilar. That is human nature. But it is sinful human nature, not human nature as redeemed by Christ, who has called his people out of "every nation, tribe, people and language" (Rev. 7:9). Later we will note some practical limitations to the application of solidarity, but the starting point is to accept our Lord's teaching that we are united with all human beings by a mutual obligation of love, concern, and help.

The error to which most Americans are prone—including American evangelicals—is the error of an overly strong emphasis on individualism. True, each of us is individually, morally responsible for our actions and choices. But it is easy to overemphasize this fact to the point that we end up denying the solidarity we all have with others.

> "Solidarity is undoubtedly a Christian virtue. . . . One's neighbor is then not only a human being with his or her own rights and a fundamental equality with everyone else, but becomes the living image of God the Father, redeemed by the blood of Jesus Christ and placed under the permanent action of the Holy Spirit. One's neighbor must therefore be loved, even if an enemy, with the same love with which the Lord loves him or her; and for that person's sake one must be ready for sacrifice, even the ultimate one: to lay down one's life for the brethren (cf. 1 John 3:16)."[3]
>
> —POPE JOHN PAUL II

A speaker addressing a student convocation of the university where I taught wanted to stress individual responsibility. He urged the students to work to get ahead by their own efforts. He said that he gained an education and achieved success in his career by his own individual efforts. Then, warming to his theme, he almost shouted, "I was born alone—as an individual—I achieved success as an individual, and I will die as an individual!" I almost leaped out of my chair to retort, "You were born alone? This is truly amazing! I heard once in human history of a virgin birth, but I have never heard of a person being born without a mother!"

Indeed, individual effort and individual responsibility are important values, but all of us are helped along our way by others. Our mothers and fathers give us birth and sacrifice to raise us. We learn from teachers and mentors who guide us. And, when our lives are over, friends and family members will gather at our bedside and hold our hands as we slip away from this life and into the arms of our Lord. It is only in solidarity with others that we can become all that God wants us to become.

Yet it is easy—and satisfying to our egos—to fall prey to an unchecked individualism. It is human nature to take credit for what we are able to achieve and to assume that others who are less successful than we are have only themselves to blame. That relieves us of any responsibility. An unchecked individualism says that we are not responsible for the problems of others. After all, I have problems of my own. Take care of number-one first of all.

I have met individuals who have tried to wiggle out of the debt of love, concern, and assistance God insists they owe others. They argue that others experiencing distress or problems suffer because of their own foolish or sinful choices. To help such victims would spare them the consequences of their actions, causing the helper to become an enabler, and would encourage the victims to continue in their self-destructive behavior. There is some truth here—but more error. Solidarity does not deny individual moral responsibility for the choices we make. At some point, when a person or an entire community persists in self-destructive behavior in spite of repeated warnings, we may need to leave them to the natural consequences of their actions. There is such a thing as tough love. More on this shortly.

But this ought not to be used as an excuse for an attitude that is as unconcerned as it is uncaring. We all have made mistakes at certain points in our lives; we all have made sinful choices. That is why the gospel of forgiveness through God's grace is indeed good news. All of us—without exception—stand in need of it. Many parents have rightly stood in solidarity with their adult children, offering help, when they find themselves in deep trouble due to foolish, even sinful choices they have made. It is the height of self-righteousness to say that anyone who has made a wrong choice forfeits his or her right to receive support and assistance from others.

In addition, often the needs and problems we face—and that some people face with overwhelming, crushing force—are not of our own making. Hurricanes, tornadoes, droughts, and other natural disasters; life-threatening illnesses; economic dislocations that throw people out of work; the actions of an oppressive, totalitarian government; the disruptions of war; religious persecution by a hateful religious majority—all are examples of conditions that can result in enormous needs and that are not due to any fault of the people suffering such calamities. The Jews of Nazi-occupied Netherlands with whom Diet and Hein stood in solidarity were caught in a web not of their own making.

Boundaries to Solidarity

Any truth taken to an extreme becomes error. That is also true of solidarity. Thus we need to think through some boundaries, or limits, to the shared responsibility for others that lies at the heart of solidarity. After all, even the Good Samaritan did not go off the route he was taking to search far and wide for additional victims of thieves he could aid, nor did he restore the goods that had been stolen. He did not promise a lifetime of care to the victim, but only enough to get him back on his feet. There are two especially important limits that put boundaries around our efforts to live in solidarity with others; these limits prevent this Christian virtue from turning into something open-ended and destructive.

A Shared Responsibility

The first limit on the application of solidarity is that *each one of us is not called to have the same depth of concern and to offer the same level of help for all people in need everywhere.* In an age of instant communication, we learn immediately of hurts and needs throughout the world, from the victims of an earthquake in Pakistan to religious persecution or starvation in Africa. Closer to home we are made aware of people being thrown out of work due to plant closings, children who are abused and neglected by their families, victims of tornadoes or hurricanes, and people struggling without proper health insurance. Does solidarity say we have an equally strong obligation to show love and concern and to offer help to all of the people in need around the globe? How do we live in solidarity with others and yet avoid being so overwhelmed with needs around the world that we give up in despair of ever making a difference?

The answer, I would suggest, lies in the combination of two principles, both of which speak to solidarity being a responsibility we share with millions of Christians around the world: a division of labor in the church and the rule of proximity. God intends for there to be a division of labor among his people. We can only do something when we do not try to do everything. The apostle Paul teaches in 1 Corinthians 12 that the church is one body made up of many parts, with each part having its special calling or gift. This means each of us is not called to be equally active in seeking to meet all needs around the world. All of us should be concerned; none of us should be indifferent. But individuals, churches, and other Christian organizations have specialized callings that differ; all do not have the same calling. Some will be called to do what they can about HIV/AIDS in Africa, others about sex trafficking in Thailand, others about spousal abuse here in the United States, others about homelessness in the local community, and yet others about a fellow church member struggling with a spouse suffering dementia. God asks all of us to have a loving concern for all people in need, but God does not expect all of us to be equally active in meeting the needs of all of them.

There is also the rule of proximity. It says that the closer God puts certain needs to us and our lives, the greater our responsibility to respond. A close friend or next-door neighbor who is battling cancer is in closer proximity than a slight acquaintance with the same disease who lives across town. When a tornado strikes one's community causing deaths, injuries, and loss of houses, the needs are in closer proximity than when a similar tornado strikes a community a thousand miles away. With greater proximity comes a greater responsibility to take action.

But we must not use this rule as an excuse for an uncaring, I'm-glad-I'm-not-affected attitude. Solidarity binds us by way of concern, prayer, and whatever help we can give—even if limited—to those who are in need, including those who are at a distance.

In addition, proximity is not always a matter of literal distance. Say a speaker comes to one's church and reports on horrendous persecution taking place against fellow Christians in a country half-way around the globe. She graphically tells of young children being kidnapped and sold into slavery, women being raped, and men being summarily executed. God, through that speaker, has suddenly placed the people of that land close to us. Their proximity is great, even though it is a distant land we may have a hard time locating on a map.

Solidarity, Yes; Paternalism, No

A second limit on the application of solidarity is rooted in *the difference between solidarity and a responsibility-denying paternalism.* God has created us to be choosing, willing, creative persons who mirror the image of God in which we have been created. This means we are morally responsible beings with the freedom to make real choices that carry with them real consequences. Solidarity does not mean others can, or should, shield us from all the consequences of our bad, sinful choices, or that we do not need to do what we can to help ourselves.

If with the best of intentions we overemphasize solidarity to the point that individuals lose sight of their responsibility for their actions and the need to do what they can for themselves, we are in danger of fostering an unhealthy dependence. That also undercuts people's God-given opportunity and obligation to be creative, willing individuals who contribute to the broader society. The wise social-service agency soon learns how to offer help to those in need without turning those recipients into people who become dependent on that help and never learn to develop their own abilities and talents. "Tough love," it is often called: It is *love* as it seeks, in solidarity with those in need, to offer help; it is *tough* as it requires people to do what they can for themselves and to increase what they can do on their own. But this ought not to be used as an excuse for an attitude of indifference. Tough love is still love. We are still seeking the best for our neighbor.

Locating the exact position of the line between paternalism and a proper acting on the basis of solidarity is not easy. It will often be in doubt, and in concrete situations equally sincere Christians will disagree on exactly where it lies. But such a line does exist, and we need, prayerfully and lovingly, to seek it.

Habitat for Humanity is a well-known Christian organization the policies of which reflect an attempt to avoid both a responsibility-denying paternalism and a solidarity-denying unconcern. It makes affordable houses available for low-income people who otherwise could not own their own homes. By the use of volunteer labor, donated building materials, and other means, the prices of the houses are brought down to the point where many families that previously could not afford their own houses now can. It has built more than two hundred thousand houses, which provide some one million people with safe, affordable housing. In doing so Habitat for Humanity acts on the basis of solidarity with those without the means to buy their own houses. But it also avoids an unbiblical paternalism. It does not simply give the houses to those in need and ask nothing in return. Those receiving the houses must make down payments and assume mortgages. They are also expected to put in hundreds of hours helping to build their own houses, which helps reduce the down payments and the monthly mortgage payments. It is an empowering program, not a giveaway program.

"Habitat is not a giveaway program. In addition to a down payment and the monthly mortgage payments, homeowners invest hundreds of hours of their own labor—sweat equity—into building their Habitat house and the houses of others."[4]

—HABITAT FOR HUMANITY FACT SHEET

So What?

Solidarity is a biblical principle crucial for guiding us in our relationships with others, and especially with those who are less well off than we are. That much is clear. However, exactly what solidarity ought to mean for us in concrete, practical terms is another question. What does solidarity mean as we seek to be a healing presence in a broken world? And what does it mean when we vote, support candidates for public office, express our opinions to family members and coworkers, and in other ways act as responsible Christian citizens?

These are the questions I will consider here. Two basic applications of the principle of solidarity can guide us. We need to examine them carefully. They may not give us complete answers to all our questions, but they will help move us closer to answers.

Solidarity May or May Not Lead to Advocating Changes in Public Policies

Standing in solidarity with those in need and advocating public policies aimed at helping them are not necessarily the same. There are many ways to show solidarity with the "least of these" (Matt. 25:45), without resorting to governmental action. We must never lose sight of this.

Churches and their members regularly offer prayers, counseling, meals, and other help to those of their members who are suffering unemployment, ill health, and bereavement. Tens of thousands of American Christians daily volunteer and give money for homeless shelters, drug addiction clinics, prisoner release programs, after-school centers, food pantries, overseas relief and development efforts, and much, much more. They are living what it means to stand in solidarity with those in need. Studies regularly show that committed Christian believers volunteer more time and give more money to agencies helping the needy than do nonbelievers. This is even true when one considers only time and money given to secular agencies helping those in need.[5]

However, this does not mean that solidarity has no consequences for us as Christian citizens as we seek to understand and evaluate public-policy questions. Sometimes solidarity will mean advocating changes in public policies.

Two experiences from my past may help illustrate a basic point. I once served on the board of a women's resource center in Los Angeles that engaged in pregnancy counseling. I was constantly moved by the women who offered counseling and help to other women who were pregnant under difficult circumstances. These counselors lived out solidarity with both the pregnant women and their unborn children. But the center neither expected nor sought government funding. It only wanted to be left alone to pursue its live-saving, help-giving work.

Another experience: Some years ago when I was serving as a state senator in Michigan, Carolyn, the sister of one of my staff members, was struck by a drunk driver as she was jogging alongside a road. Severely injured, she spent weeks in the hospital and in rehabilitation, and ultimately was permanently disabled. It turned out the driver who hit her had previously killed someone else while driving drunk. Yet the drunk driver was out of jail on bail before Carolyn was out of the hospital!

How could I best live out the Christian principle of solidarity in a situation such as this? Surely offering prayers and showing concern for Carolyn and other victims of drunk drivers would be appropriate. Whatever concrete, practical help I could offer would be called for. But I concluded that to stop there would not have been enough. Weak anti-drunk-driving laws and their inconsistent enforcement were a big part of the problem. Public policies needed to change. Thus I introduced in the legislature a package of anti-drunk-driving bills that, with the strong help of Mothers against Drunk Driving, eventually passed. Since then much has changed, so that both public attitudes and the judicial system now see drunk driving as a truly serious crime.

These two events from my past illustrate that sometimes living out the principle of solidarity will lead to advocating changed public policies and sometimes it will not. Much depends on circumstances and opportunities.

We should never shrug off our responsibility to act in solidarity with our neighbors—wherever they may be—by assuming it is the government's job to deal with their problems and needs. Nevertheless, in certain circumstances government actions are needed. Then living in solidarity with others needs to take the form of us as citizens asking our government to take certain steps. Remember, God established government to promote greater justice in a broken world. Three situations when we ought to turn to government readily come to mind.

One such situation is when our sense of solidarity is calling us to act on behalf of others in need—yet public policies themselves are causing or contributing to those needs. Sometimes public policies are the problem. To minister to those in need without working to change public policies that are causing their needs is to treat the symptoms without dealing with the root causes. For example, some states pay for women receiving welfare assistance to obtain abortions but refuse to increase their welfare benefits if they give birth. Such states thereby create a strong financial incentive for women receiving welfare benefits to obtain abortions. In such a situation, the only direct, truly effective way to act in solidarity with those suffering the consequences of such public policies is to work to change those policies.

A second situation where solidarity leads to a concern with public policies is rooted in how a government elsewhere in the world treats its people. In early 2006 Abdul Rahman, a citizen of Afghanistan who had converted from Islam to Christianity, was in the news. He had been arrested for becoming a Christian and was threatened with execution.[6] Following an international outcry and protests by the American government, he was released and allowed to leave Afghanistan. It is hard to see how private, nongovernmental action could have had the same results.

Another example: In recent years genocide has taken place in the Darfur region of Sudan. The central government has looked the other way and perhaps even encouraged Arab extremists who are conducting a systematic campaign of killing, raping, and looting. The American government declared this a situation of genocide. In the early years of the twenty-first century, this is probably the most egregious case of wonton death. We need to stand in solidarity with the suffering people of Darfur. But we all feel helpless in the face of a catastrophe taking place half a world away. There may be some things we can do through private relief agencies, but the most effective action we can take is to urge our government to take up the cause of the residents of Darfur in the United Nations and to bring direct pressures to bear on the Sudanese government.

Private and group efforts—as good as they may be—are sometimes inadequate to meet certain needs in a community. This leads to the third situation where solidarity may call for us to work for changes in public policies. When private and group efforts are inadequate to meet a need, their efforts can often best be combined with those of the government and its public policies. Think of a program that is run by a group of Christians deeply concerned with the plight of the homeless in their city, especially families. The program may succeed in finding and rehabilitating a large home that provides living quarters for the homeless, and it may establish training programs

designed to get at the root causes of the homeless condition. I have
visited such programs and have been deeply moved by the dedica-
tion and love shown by program staff and volunteers. But often the
program leaders themselves are the first to admit that they are only
scratching the surface of the overall problem. They can only help
some. For each one helped there are many more in their cities they
are unable to help.

Staff members have expressed two desires to me. One is that
they receive some government funding without interference with
their programming and without time-consuming paperwork. The
second is that the government would pursue policies to reduce
the incidence of homelessness in their city. Better schools, drug
treatment for all those who wish it, better prisoner re-entry programs, improved employment-training programs, and stronger
public-transit systems so people can get to jobs outside their own
neighborhoods—these are all desires I have heard expressed. We
can question which of such public-policy programs would be most
effective in reducing homelessness in our cities, but they illustrate
that public policies and Christ-motivated acts of solidarity with
the homeless—as well as many others facing severe needs—can
often best be addressed by both public-policy changes and private
actions.

Solidarity Leads to Justice and the Common Good

There is a second key, practical application of the principle of
solidarity. Solidarity means Christian citizens should think and act,
not in terms of their own self-interest and their own needs, but of
justice for all and the promotion of the common good. In the previous chapter I discussed justice and the common good. One can say
that solidarity is the gasoline that fuels our drive to seek justice and
the common good. Based on solidarity with our neighbors, we should
care passionately about securing greater justice for them. This sounds
simple, but it in fact is revolutionary.

Candidates for public office are notorious for appealing to our
self-interest. They sometimes ask the voters if they are better off
than they were four years ago. The implication is that if the answer
is yes, they should return the incumbents to power; if the answer is

no, they should elect a new set of office holders. But in either case the hidden assumption is that how one votes ought to be based on how one personally, as an individual, is doing financially. How our neighbors—whom we have been commanded to love as ourselves—are doing does not enter in at all.

Members of Congress constantly seek to garner votes by pointing to spending programs they have secured for their home districts. "Bringing home the bacon," it is called. Members of Congress are expected to fight to keep open military installations in their home areas, whether or not they are needed for national defense, even if closing the bases would save millions of dollars. We as consumers are promised tax cuts or cheaper gasoline; employers are promised cheap labor; workers are promised a higher minimum wage or protection against overseas imports; senior citizens are promised protected Social Security benefits; parents are promised better schools. I have sat in on campaign strategy sessions where the typical approach is to divide the voters into a series of ethnic, regional, and economic interests and then figure out how to appeal to the self-interest of each. But this is the way of the world, not God's way.

We Christians ought to be insulted by such appeals to our self-interest. As responsible Christian citizens—motivated by our solidarity with our fellow human beings—we need to ask questions about the common good, not our own personal good. Solidarity with our neighbors, especially with those with special needs, requires no less.

An unchecked self-interest that is all too evident in the United States—and also in our churches—deserves condemnation. Typically, when do people become politically active and involved? Only when something near and dear to them personally is threatened. I have seen this time and time again. And that is not right. For the Christian, self-interest—whether individual or group—must never be the driving motivation for political involvement. We need to work, self-consciously and persistently, to avoid the trap of self-interest as the driving force for our voting, writing letters, and other acts of citizen involvement. Yet self-interest is an ever-present force, somewhat like the air we breathe. That makes it easy not even to notice it. It comes to appear natural; it's just the way things are. No one expects things to be different. That is why it takes self-conscious, persistent efforts, and much prayer and the help of fellow Christians to lay aside self-interest and substitute solidarity as the driving force in our lives as citizens.

Conclusion

Underlying Christians' work to redeem a fallen world and to work for justice and the common good is the command to love our neighbors as ourselves, that is, the principle of solidarity. Sometimes solidarity will drive us to our knees in prayer, sometimes to giving our money to organizations offering help in Christ's name, sometimes to direct, personal acts of comfort and help, and sometimes to supporting public policies that oppose wrongs and promote greater justice. And sometimes it will lead us to pursue all four together.

Questions for Reflection and Discussion

1. What if television or your local newspaper carried a story about thousands of young children being orphaned due to the HIV/ AIDS epidemic in many parts of Africa? How would two different individuals, one guided by solidarity and the other by individualism, react to this news story? Is solidarity or individualism a better guide to a Christian reaction? Give reasons for your answer.

2. How do you—and how *should* you—decide what individuals with needs God is asking you to help and what individuals, who may have equally great needs, God is not asking you to help?

3. It is important for Christians to express solidarity with those in need by giving concrete help and at the same time avoiding a paternalism that stifles initiative and rewards wrong choices. Do you sometimes struggle to know how much and what sort of help you ought to give someone you know (a family member, a fellow church member, a neighbor)? How do you—and how should you—determine exactly what solidarity with that person means in that situation?

4. This chapter argues that Christian citizens best live out the principle of solidarity by sometimes working to change government and its public policies and sometimes by engaging in private, nongovernmental actions. From your own experience or from news stories, identify (1) an example of a situation in which solidarity might lead Christians to work to change public policies and (2) an example of a situation in which solidarity might lead Christians to act individually or as a group and not through government.

5

Civil Society

*"Present Yourselves before the Lord
by Your Tribes and Clans"*

(1 S a m u e l 1 0 : 1 9)

THE CLASSIC **1964** MOVIE *BECKET* portrays actual twelfth-century events
surrounding King Henry II of England, played by Peter O'Toole, and
the archbishop of Canterbury, Thomas à Becket, played by Richard
Burton. The two were close friends and confidants. When the archbishop of Canterbury—the head of the English church—dies, Henry
appoints Becket as the new archbishop, thinking he could trust him
to go along with his wishes. But Thomas à Becket, impressed with
the awesome responsibility he has been given, experiences the redeeming grace of God, gives away his possessions to the poor, and
seeks humbly to serve Christ's church.

This leads him into a conflict with King Henry over the question
of whether or not the king's civil courts had jurisdiction over priests.
Henry, in frustration and anger, expresses his desire to be rid of the
now Christlike Becket, who insists the civil government has no authority over the church and its affairs. Some of Henry's nobles take
this as their cue, ride to Canterbury, and kill Becket in cold blood.

Even today visitors to Canterbury Cathedral are shown the side door where on December 29, 1170, Thomas à Becket was killed.

Fast forward more than eight hundred years to 2006. Ray and Sharon Rivera of El Paso, Texas, had been home schooling their daughter for five years. One day a truant officer appeared at their door and demanded they place their child in a local public school. The next day an "at-risk coordinator" from the public schools came by and told the Riveras they immediately had to put their daughter in school. Later a police officer showed up at their door with a summons to appear in court in two days. When they did so, the judge exclaimed, "Who in their right mind would home school their children?" He went on to question whether the child was being harmed by being isolated from other children. But the Riveras carefully explained how they went about home schooling their daughter, pointed out the many social contacts she had with her peers, and showed the judge the books they used and some exercises their child had completed. The judge ended up dismissing the case.[1]

These two stories—although dealing with very different events separated by more than eight centuries—concern the same issue: In the final analysis does the government possess all authority, with churches, families, and other social institutions having only what responsibilities the government decides to give them? Or have they been given responsibilities and authority directly by God himself upon which no government may trespass? Becket paid with his life for insisting that the church receives its authority directly from God, not from the government. And the Riveras were hauled into court, because they insisted they—and not the government—had the right to decide how their daughter was to be educated and trained. Both Becket and the Riveras insisted God had given them distinct responsibilities—as the leader of the church in Becket's case and as parents in the Riveras' case—and no one other than God had a right to tell them how they were to fulfill that responsibility. They were kings, so to speak, in the positions God had given them.

To have a Christian perspective on governments and the public policies they adopt it is important to understand that American society—as any society—is made up of more than the government and individuals. Liberals tend to focus on government and its society-wide public policies; conservatives tend to focus on free individuals operating in a free market. Both can forget there is much more to society than the government and individuals. A host of social institutions and organizations lies between government and the individual: families, churches, nonprofit organizations, self-help groups, recreation clubs, sports leagues, art organizations, voluntary associations, and many more. Social institutions and organizations such as these are referred to as civil society.

In this chapter I first consider more precisely what is meant by civil society. Next I consider indications from the Bible that the institutions of civil society are a part of God's will for human society. They receive their right to exist and their authority not from government, but from God himself. Finally, I consider why these ideas are important to understand before we embark on our journey of exploring a number of today's specific, concrete public-policy questions.

Civil Society

In August 2005 Hurricane Katrina slammed into New Orleans and other areas of the Gulf Coast, leaving staggering destruction in its wake. More than fifteen hundred lives were lost, property damage was beyond reckoning, and hundreds of thousands were left homeless. There are three ways in which communities can respond to devastation on this scale. One could be called the rugged-individual approach. Under it individuals should grit their teeth, get to work, and provide for themselves. A second response is what could be called the welfare-state response. People—in face of overwhelming needs and feelings of impotence—expect the government to come in and meet all their needs. But there is a third approach. This is the civil-society approach. It looks to family members, churches, neighbors, and voluntary disaster-relief agencies for needed help.[2]

In actual practice when natural disasters strike, communities usually do not turn only to one of these approaches but look to a combination of them. There are things people can and should do to help themselves, government and its emergency relief agencies have a role to play, and private relief agencies such as the Red Cross and church-based emergency response teams also have something to contribute. These three responses to a natural disaster help illustrate that in seeking a more just society marked by shalom, the role to be played by civil society ought not to be ignored.

The fact is that we do not live our lives as separate, isolated individuals. Nor do we only live them as a part of large, impersonal bureaucratic structures such as giant corporations and modern government. Instead, all of us are woven into a network of human relationships—into families, groups of friends, local congregations, neighborhoods, clubs, self-help and support groups, and more. Some would also include small, local businesses. This is civil society. Excluded are the large, impersonal, bureaucratic structures of modern society; included are the personal, more human groupings within which we live day to day.

"Hours after Hurricane Katrina's fury subsided, faith-based groups were on the scene, providing desperately needed help in the emergency rescue and relief operations, all as part of their religious mission."[3]

—KIM LAWTON, REPORTER FOR THE *RELIGION AND ETHICS NEWSWEEKLY*

Why is civil society important? First of all, because it is within civil society that we learn the beliefs and attitudes that shape our lives. Here we learn such virtues as honesty and integrity, faithfulness in marriage, and respect for others who differ from us in race, ethnicity, or religion.

Second, civil society is important because its institutions and associations themselves meet many needs we all have. Families nurture, support, and train children. Local congregations meet the religious needs of their members and offer emotional and physical support in times of crisis, such as unemployment, divorce, sickness, and death. Neighborhood groups work to prevent crime, eliminate drug dealing, and stem deterioration. Clubs such as Rotary and Kiwanis provide community-building services. As in the Katrina example, voluntary relief agencies provide emergency help and rebuilding assistance in times of natural disasters.

All this deeply affects public policies, which emerge out of the beliefs and attitudes shaped by civil society. As civil society meets needs that are present in society, there is less need for public policies to respond to them—or the responses will be quite different.

But from a Christian perspective, much more needs to be said about the institutions and groups that make up civil society. They are not simply an accidental feature of twenty-first-century American life. Instead, they are a part of God's ordering of his creation. The next section explores why this is the case.

Civil Society as Part of God's Order for Society

In 1863 a young Dutch pastor named Abraham Kuyper, fresh out of seminary, accepted a position as minister of a church in the small village of Beesd.[4] He had been trained in the fashionable tradition of a genial, liberal theology prominent in the state-supported church of his day. As a young pastor in a new church, he made the rounds of his congregation's members, calling on them in their homes. One of the members on whom he called was Pietje Baltus, a simple, uneducated woman in her thirties, but a strong woman whose deep Christian faith was rooted in God's Word. What had been intended to be a polite visit soon turned into Baltus's searching questions concerning the state of the young pastor's own soul. She told of her deep convictions and the sure hope for eternal life they gave her, and she warned the young pastor his own soul could be in danger. This got Kuyper thinking. He returned often to visit with Baltus and other parishioners of similar convictions. Eventually, for the first time in his life, he confessed Jesus Christ as his own personal Savior from sin and fully dedicated his life to him.

> "Before I knew it, I was kneeling in front of my chair with folded hands. Oh, what my soul experienced at that moment I fully understood only later. Yet, from that moment on I despised what I used to admire and I sought what I had dared to despise!"[5]
>
> —ABRAHAM KUYPER,
> DUTCH PASTOR AND PRIME MINISTER,
> RECOUNTING HIS CONVERSION

Abraham Kuyper went on to found a Christian university and a newspaper, write countless books and essays, engage in Dutch politics, and serve as prime minister of the Netherlands. He was one of the most influential Christian voices in the Netherlands at the beginning of the twentieth century. Today his books and speeches continue to be read and to exert an influence in both Europe and the United States. There is much we can still learn from Abraham Kuyper.

Central to Kuyper's thinking was a basic Christian idea that has gone by different names that are sufficient to scare away all but the most dedicated readers. Kuyper refers to it as "sphere sovereignty" and Catholic social teaching refers to largely the same idea as "subsidiarity."[6] As imposing as these labels are, the basic underlying idea is not difficult to grasp and is an important guide to public policies that are limited in nature yet pursue the justice for which the Bible fervently calls. There are two basic steps to understanding it.

Societies Consist of Distinct Institutions and Organizations

Genesis 2:18 relates that, at the dawn of human history after creating Adam, God declared: "It is not good for the man to be alone." It was then that God created Eve—another human being created in God's image—and in her Adam found the partner for whom he had longed (Gen. 2:22–24). Adam's need for society, for others, was now satisfied.

The Bible teaches that God did not create human beings as separate, distinct individuals whom he intended to live in isolation from others. No, he made us to be social beings. We need others and find fulfillment only in conjunction with others.

The family was a part of this: "For this reason a man will leave his father and mother and be united to his wife, and they will become one flesh" (Gen. 2:24). The Old Testament laws governing divorce and Christ's reinforcement of those laws add to the biblical witness of the importance of marriage and the family in God's plan for human society (Deut. 24:1–4; Matt. 5:31–32). But that is only the beginning of the Bible's witness to our social nature.

Throughout the Bible God worked primarily through human groups and organizations, not through solitary individuals. He called Abraham and Sarah, gave them a son, and made a great nation out of them. He worked through that nation throughout the Old Testament. Ancient Israel was, in turn, organized into tribes and clans, as the subtitle of this chapter relates. Jesus Christ called out a band of twelve disciples through whom he worked. He established a church, a body of believers. The book of Acts relates the history of the early church, not the history of individual believers: on Pentecost the Holy Spirit was sent to a collection of people who were gathered together, church councils were held, and Paul was part of a team on his missionary journeys (Acts 2:1; 13:2–3; 15:1–35, 40).

"American men, women, and children are members of many communities—families; neighborhoods; innumerable social, religious, ethnic, workplace, and professional associations; and the body politic itself. Neither human existence nor individual liberty can be sustained for long outside the interdependent and overlapping communities to which all of us belong."[7]

—THE COMMUNITARIAN PLATFORM

Simple observation tells us that wherever human societies exist, groups such as families, clans, villages, and religious organizations also are present. In the United States we raise children, pursue economic activities, worship God, and recreate, not as isolated individuals, but as members of groups. There are families, schools, business corporations, churches, neighborhood associations, soccer leagues, and more. These are what make up civil society.

The various organizations and institutions that comprise civil society are neither accidental nor mere conveniences that could be done away with if times change and some other way of organizing society develops. They are a necessary, inherent, God-intended part of human society as God created it.

Institutions and Organizations Possess Distinct, God-Given Responsibilities

Remember Abraham Kuyper, the Dutch theologian, politician, author, and pastor? What he called "sphere sovereignty" insisted, as we just saw, that the social institutions and organizations that make up civil society are an inherent, God-intended feature of human society. The second step in his thinking is that they possess their own God-given responsibilities. He taught that what he called "spheres"—fields or areas of human activity such as marriage and the family, religion and the church, education and schools, and artistic endeavors and art organizations—were all areas with their own, distinct responsibilities. Their responsibilities come from God, not from government. No government, no public policy may dictate how the institutions in these various areas are to fulfill their responsibilities.

I need to make an important qualification to this basic point. In no way do I mean that people may do whatever they please in fulfilling the responsibilities that they have been given by God. In a broken, sinful world, people can act in an inappropriate, unloving manner. I'll discuss this more later. But for now what I need to emphasize is that the various social institutions receive from God the right, the authority, to play a distinctive role in the area or sphere in which they have responsibilities.

This means that in a very real sense the government is not over the family. Each has been instituted by God; each has its own, distinct responsibilities where it has the right to act without the interference or dictates of other institutions. The family was instituted not by government, but by God. Public policies ought not to dictate how a mother and father raise their children: what rules to establish, what values to instill, and what education to give them.

Similarly the government is to stay out of the affairs of the church. Nor should government dictate what constitutes good art or good literature or interfere with academic freedom in colleges and universities. All these institutions have as much right to exist as does the government; all are institutions that have areas or fields (spheres) where they should be free to act without public policies dictating what they must and must not do. Especially the family and the church, but also education, labor, business, art, and literature, are all part of God's will for human societies; all receive their purpose and meaning from God; all have as much right to exist in freedom and independence as does government.

Therefore Thomas à Becket was right to resist what he saw as King Henry's encroachment onto the church's responsibilities. And the Riveras were right to resist their school district's attempts to force them to discontinue the home schooling of their child and send her to the public schools.

The Roman Catholic tradition often refers to the idea of subsidiarity, which is similar to what I have been describing. It also recognizes a plurality of societal institutions and organizations in society. It then goes on to add the helpful insight that social tasks should be performed on the lowest level consistent with a just order and the common good. It insists that local organizations should not do what the family can do, regional organizations and local governments should not do what local organizations can do, and national organizations and governments should not do what regional organizations and local governments can do. Higher, more inclusive social institutions should not try to take over and perform the responsibilities that belong to lower, less inclusive social institutions.

An Important Qualification

On January 11, 2006, the body of a seven-year-old girl, Nixzmary Brown, was found in her family's Brooklyn apartment. Officials reported she had been killed when her stepfather banged her head against a faucet in the bathtub. They found she had been repeatedly beaten by her stepfather. The prosecutor in the case reported, "There was barely a spot on this child that was not marked by her parents."[8] Too often we hear of similar tragic incidences: a child is left alone for days while the mother or father is off drinking or gambling, or a child is subjected to sexual abuse by a live-in boyfriend of the mother.

What are we to say to tragedies such as this? Does the concept of the family with a distinct, God-given role to play, as a separate "sphere" in which government and its public policies are not to interfere, mean the government should take no action? Or what if a religious cult uses psychological pressure to win converts and keep them under its spell? Should the government take no action against such a cult, because of the principle of the state not interfering in the affairs of the church?

To such questions I answer, "Definitely not!" What I have thus far written has looked at only one side of a coin. It is now time to turn the coin over, and examine its other side. Doing so will lead to an important qualification.

As we saw in previous chapters, governments have the awesome task of restraining the effects of sin in a broken world by seeking justice and promoting the common good. This means there are two dangers: (1) of governments sitting by passively while gross injustices are committed, and (2) of governments too quickly and easily interfering in the activities of families, churches, or other societal institutions.

There are many examples of governments that have steered into the ditch on either one side or the other of the road. I can think of instances when our own government did not take action when it should have. Until the 1960s our government ignored and even participated in the violation of the basic, God-given human rights of African Americans. For years Congress refused to pass legislation even making lynching a federal crime. Or one can think of the Sago Mine disaster in West Virginia that killed twelve coal miners in 2006, after repeated safety violations noted by government inspectors had gone uncorrected.

Government has the awesome, God-given duty to promote justice and seek the common good in a broken, sinful world. When the other social institutions are not properly fulfilling their God-given responsibilities, but instead are acting in an unjust, hurtful manner, government has a duty to intervene.

But government has sometimes veered off into the opposite ditch—that of interfering in the actions of civil-society institutions and organizations when it ought not to have done so. One can cite the state of Oregon whose voters in 1922 passed a law prohibiting parents from sending their children to private schools and requiring them to attend public schools. This legislation interfered with the right of parents to educate their children in keeping with their religious faith. Happily the United States Supreme Court ruled in 1925 that Oregon had violated the right of parents "to direct the upbringing and education of children under their control." Today some states and local school districts, as we saw in the case of the Riveras, have harassed parents who have wished to home school their children.

"We think it entirely plain that the Act of 1922 unreasonably interferes with the liberty of parents and guardians to direct the upbringing and education of children under their control. . . . The child is not the mere creature of the state; those who nurture him and direct his destiny have the right, coupled with the high duty, to recognize and prepare him for additional obligations."[9]

—JAMES C. MCREYNOLDS, UNITED STATES SUPREME COURT JUSTICE

So What?

The idea of civil society's social institutions being God-established and having distinct, God-willed responsibilities has practical, immediate, here-and-now consequences for public policies. There are three especially important implications for public policies and our understanding of them.

Take Civil Society into Consideration

The first implication is that *public policies should respect, make room for, and make use of the institutions of civil society*. A Christian approach to public-policy questions seeks to honor and give due respect to those civil-society institutions that lie between the individual and the national government. Government is surely important and a part of God's ordering of his creation. The individual is also of great importance in God's sight. But social groups and institutions—and especially the family and the church—are also a part of God's ordering of human society.

This means that whenever a new public policy is proposed we need to ask whether or not it will ignore, harm, or undercut existing social institutions such as the family, private schools, churches, self-help and voluntary groups, and local governing units. Often environmental impact statements are required when new actions of the government might harm the natural environment. It would be equally appropriate to require "civil-society impact statements." Citizens and decision makers ought to be aware of the impact of their actions on the many social groups and institutions that make up civil society. We must be careful that the public policies we adopt do not harm them and make the good work they are doing in society more difficult.

It is easy for public policies—whether inadvertently or purposefully—to interfere with the goals and freedoms of families, private schools, churches, faith-based social-service agencies, and other religious or secular social groups and institutions. Think of government-sponsored schools—the public schools and state universities—that may present a distorted view of Christianity and undercut what families are trying to teach their children. Think of local zoning ordinances that have sometimes prevented a church from expanding, to accommodate its increasing numbers of congregants. Or think of a Christian drug-treatment center that is required to hire staff members without regard to their religious faith. There have been cases when zoning ordinances have been used to block churches from feeding the poor in their church buildings.

Not only should public policies avoid harming existing social institutions, but—when appropriate and workable—they should work with them to achieve a more just order in society. With some financial help, for example, a church-run, prisoner re-entry program may be able to help prisoners make the difficult transition from prison life to becoming productive members of the community. It may even do so for less money and more effectively than the traditional, government-run corrections and parole system. The ex-offenders benefit, a public program is relieved of some of its responsibilities, and society gains as the people being helped are less likely to become repeat offenders. The church and its re-entry program—social institutions that are a part of civil society—are affirmed and strengthened, not ignored or undercut by the government.

President George W. Bush's faith-based and community initiative fits into this pattern. It has attempted to enable faith-based and small, community-oriented organizations to compete for government funds on an equal basis with their larger counterparts. When government works through these agencies, government is relieved of providing services directly. Doing so also reinforces and expands the positive work localized, private social-service agencies are doing.

Here the idea that subsidiarity stresses—that tasks should be performed on the lowest level that is effective—has many practical implications for public policy. Whenever a new task for government is proposed, subsidiarity asks whether that task could be performed by a private agency better than by government. Or could it be performed by a local government or a private regional agency better than by a state government agency? Or by a state government agency better than by a federal government agency?

Both liberals and conservatives often overlook the importance of civil-society groups and institutions that lie between the individual and the government. When that happens, the only alternatives, when a need or problem is identified, are to leave individuals to struggle alone to meet that need or problem or to shift responsibilities to the government and its large, often inflexible bureaucracies. Neither is ideal.

Active yet Limited Government

A second implication of a biblical view of civil society is that public policy should make an effort to strike *a balance between active, involved government and limited government.* Government is a God-intended means of redeeming life in a broken world and of pursuing justice and the common good. It is one way to live the Christian ideal of solidarity. I discussed these ideas in prior chapters. They suggest that government is to play a significant role in society.

But the idea of civil society introduced in this chapter speaks clearly and explicitly of limited government. Government's authority is broad and God-given; it is also limited. Government has its sphere in which it is to operate, but the social institutions of civil society also have their spheres in which they are to operate free of an intrusive, oppressive government. Government is only to interfere when justice and the common good require it to do so. Biblical principles support both an active, involved government and a limited government.

We as Christian citizens are called to seek—thoughtfully and prayerfully—the appropriate, justice-promoting balance between active and limited government. This is not easy. There will be many borderline cases, where reasonable people will disagree on whether government is being too passive or too aggressive in exercising its God-given authority. We will run into some of these borderline cases in later chapters. This is where prayer, careful reflection, and the help and insight of fellow believers should come into play.

Accepting Societal Diversity

A third, and final, implication of a Christian understanding of the nature and importance of civil society is *a need to accept differences and diversity in society.* In chapter 3 we saw that when public policies pursue justice as their goal, some people will use the resulting freedom and opportunities in ways that are contrary to God's will. That same observation is true in regard to limited government that respects the rights of local and regional associations and social institutions to live and act in freedom. Some will use that freedom to act in ways that will strike us as odd at best and at worst as destructive of values we hold dear.

One organization in civil society is the Freedom from Religion Foundation, whose Web site proclaims the following nonsense: "There is no greater source of strife, hatred, terrorism, bloodshed, persecution or war than religion."[10] Also included in civil society is the "Witches Voice," which identifies itself as "Neopagan news/networking on the net since 1997."[11]

What attitude ought Christians to hold in the light of this sort of diversity? Is tolerance in the face of social institutions marked by unchristian attitudes and practices in our society a virtue or a fault? We should *not* be tolerant in the sense of saying that differences in beliefs and practices do not matter. They matter, and they matter deeply. Surely it is not intolerant to disagree strongly and voice that disagreement clearly to those we believe are in the wrong.

But as we voice our disagreements, we should not try to use the power of government to shut down or put at a disadvantage those organizations in civil society with which we disagree. This point is similar to the one I made in regard to applying the ideal of justice. Justice means freedom. When applied to the institutions found in civil society, it means they have as much right to exist and speak as do we. Those who have sadly concluded that all religion is false and a source of strife or those who have given themselves over to pagan beliefs are tragically, disastrously wrong. But we are to win them by love and obedience, not the force of law. "Live such good lives among the pagans that, though they accuse you of doing wrong, they may see your good deeds and glorify God on the day he visits us" (1 Peter 2:12).

Also, when we oppose those with whom we disagree, it is important to speak "the truth in love" (Eph. 4:15). Speaking the truth in love in a society made up of diverse social institutions and organizations means that when we disagree with others we voice that disagreement in a respectful manner.

Christians have sometimes treated people with whom they disagree in a disrespectful manner. I have blushed at some of the comments made by my fellow evangelicals about gay-rights activists, political liberals, and organizations such as the American Civil Liberties Union. Part of the price of our freedom is to treat all people with respect, even while strongly disagreeing with them and clearly voicing that disagreement. And we should do so even when we have not been treated with respect by them. In doing so we set an example of what freedom is all about and live up to our Lord's command to "bless those who curse you, pray for those who mistreat you" (Luke 6:28).

Forbearance is another Christian virtue we need to follow. (See 1 Corinthians 8 and Romans 14.) We have become, as it is often put, a litigious society. People are quick to sue someone else to right a perceived wrong. If all people, including Christians, insist that every wrong done them must be publicly recognized, apologized for, and made right, there will be no end to conflict and bitterness. We all sometimes suffer wrongs—whether at work, in our marriages, at school, in the clubs to which we belong, and, yes, at church. We also, often unknowingly, wrong others.

We live in an imperfect world where life is not always fair. If we as a society are to have the unity needed to make thousands or millions of people living in a geographic area into a true society, we need sometimes to accept a certain unfairness and move on. Christians should exemplify this virtue. Remember we have been instructed to lend to people "without expecting to get anything back" (Luke 6:35) and to be wronged rather than take fellow believers into court (1 Cor. 6:7).

Conclusion

In the previous four chapters, we have considered a number of key biblical principles that are relevant to the world of public-policy issues and controversies. I promised that what may have seemed to be abstract theory does in fact have practical applications to the down-to-earth world of public policies. In the next seven chapters, we will turn to those concrete public policies that divide us as Americans and, often, even as Christian citizens.

Questions for Reflection and Discussion

1. Name some civil-society institutions or organizations of which you are a part. How important are they to you? How would your life change if they were no longer a part of your life?

2. Think again about the civil-society institutions and organizations you named in question 1. Describe responsibilities you believe God has given them to fulfill in society; that is, what their God-given purpose or role is.

3. Describe any civil-society institutions of which you are aware that are being improperly interfered with by government and its public policies.

4. Describe any civil-society institutions that could potentially benefit from financial or other assistance from public policies.

5. Are you bothered by the fact that in civil society there may be Islamic or atheistic organizations and other organizations with which you deeply disagree? Do you and your Christian values feel threatened by them? Should you feel threatened by them? Explain.

PART TWO

APPLICATIONS

6

Church and State

*"Give to Caesar What Is Caesar's,
and to God What Is God's"*

(M a t t h e w   2 2 : 2 1)

IN 2003 A CONTROVERSY AROSE IN ALABAMA that made headlines nationwide and was the lead story on CNN. The chief justice of the Alabama Supreme Court, Roy S. Moore, installed a two-and-a-half-ton granite monument in the rotunda of the state judicial building with the Ten Commandments carved on it. A United States District Court judge ruled that the monument was an endorsement of religion in violation of the First Amendment of the Constitution. He ordered the monument removed. Moore refused, declaring, "God has chosen this time and this place so we can save our country and save our courts for our children." Alabama's judicial ethics panel reacted by removing Judge Moore from office for his refusal to obey a clear court order.[1]

Another event: In the 1990s in an effort to create a lively exchange of ideas and opinions, the University of Virginia subsidized student publications. It subsidized fifteen different publications, ranging from an environmental publication to *Yellow Journal*, featuring antireligious tirades. Ronald Rosenberger and several other evangelical students started a publication called *Wide Awake*, in which they discussed from a clearly Christian perspective a number of current issues, such as war and peace, eating disorders, and homosexuality.

Wide Awake was denied university funding. Why? Because it was a religious publication, and the university had a policy against funding religious student publications. The students took their case to the courts. The lower federal courts sided with the university, but in a razor-thin, five to four decision, the United States Supreme Court ruled in favor of the evangelical students. The Court stated that the First Amendment's guarantee of governmental neutrality on matters of religion "is respected, not offended, when the government, following neutral criteria and evenhanded policies, extends benefits to recipients whose ideologies and viewpoints, including religious ones, are broad and diverse."[2]

In effect, the Supreme Court ruled that the University of Virginia could fund all legitimate student publications or no student publications; what it could not do is fund the secular ones but not the religious ones. To do so would discriminate against religious viewpoints.

What do these two events teach us about the relationship between church and state? How should we evangelical Christians—who take the Bible seriously and seek to live it out as citizens—react to the Judge Moores and Ronald Rosenbergers of this world? Salute them as heroes of faith? Or condemn them for trying to prop up their faith with governmental support?

This chapter first considers a very basic principle that will help guide us through the church-state maze; it next compares two approaches to religious freedom issues. Then we will be ready to return to Judge Moore and Ronald Rosenberger and the stands they took and look at three other pressing, puzzling church-state issues—ones that prompt clashing opinions by many evangelicals.

A Basic Principle

What is religious freedom? If asked this question by some TV news crew doing on-the-street interviews, many of us would answer something to the effect that freedom of religion means the ability to worship God as we see fit. And we would not be far off.

Freedom of religion means being able to worship God and follow one's conscience and beliefs without fear of arrest and repression by the government. At heart, this is what the not-fully-clear words of the First Amendment of the Constitution are about: "Congress shall make no law respecting an establishment of religion, or prohibiting the free exercise thereof." Freedom of religion as provided in the First Amendment means being free to worship God as one's conscience dictates—or to worship no God at all.

Here we need to recall from earlier chapters the biblical principles of justice as the God-given purpose of governments, of solidarity as being a duty all Christians share, and of civil-society organizations as being a part of God's will for human society.

A government seeking *justice* for all its citizens will neither try to prevent anyone from worshiping God as one's conscience dictates, nor try to force anyone to worship God (or gods) in ways contrary to his or her conscience or beliefs. A violation of religious freedom—and thereby of the principle of justice—can take the form of outright governmental coercion, but it is more likely to

> "What our Constitution indispensably protects is the freedom of each of us, be he Jew or Agnostic, Christian or Atheist, Buddhist or Freethinker, to believe or disbelieve, to worship or not worship, to pray or keep silent, according to his own conscience, uncoerced and unrestrained by government."[3]
>
> —POTTER STEWART, UNITED STATES SUPREME COURT JUSTICE

take the form of gentler practices that give advantages or disadvantages to certain religious beliefs—or to nonreligious, secular belief systems. Perhaps the most basic right of all that is due us is the right to worship God as our conscience demands.

Solidarity demands that we be concerned with the violation of religious-freedom rights, even when we ourselves are not affected. This will sometimes be harder to do than what we might think. It is easy for us to defend the religious-freedom rights of ourselves and of our fellow Christians. But solidarity with all our neighbors demands that we be as concerned for the religious freedom of our Jewish, Muslim, and unbelieving neighbors as we are for our own. Recall Diet Eman and Hein Seitsma, who in Nazi-occupied Netherlands were willing to put their lives at risk to protect their Jewish neighbors. Hein paid with his life in the Dachau concentration camp. Most of us are asked to do much less. But we ought to speak up if our non-Christian fellow citizens and their religious beliefs and practices are being put at a disadvantage due to our government's public policies—even as we witness to them of Christ's love and pray that they too may some day come to accept Christ's offer of salvation.

The vision of full religious freedom is also in keeping with the God-willed importance of *civil society*. Remember Abraham Kuyper? Churches, synagogues, and mosques are civil-society institutions that have a God-given sovereignty in their "spheres." Government should not intrude into the business of religious congregations, either to help or to hinder. That most definitely is not the role of government.

Thus a justice-promoting, solidarity-motivated, civil-society-respecting approach to religious freedom means public policies ought to be evenhanded or neutral toward those of all faiths and of none. That means we as Christians ought not to claim any special privileges or advantages over our neighbors who hold other religious beliefs or none at all. Our solidarity with them demands this. Claiming special advantages would be falling into the Christian-nation trap I first discussed in chapter 1. But evenhanded public policies also mean our non-Christian neighbors ought not to be given any special privileges or advantages over us who are Christians. This principle of evenhandedness is fundamental. One needs to get it right in order to get today's specific church-state controversies right.

More specific insights, however, are needed. I will soon be discussing such issues as the posting of the Ten Commandments in public places, school prayer, and government-issued vouchers to pay for education at home or in Christian schools. To do so we need to discuss more concrete ideas. Two are especially important. I consider them in the next section.

Church-State Separation versus Evenhandedness

There are those who argue that the way to achieve religious freedom for all, as I have been describing it, is by strictly separating church and state. They say the way to assure that public policies play no favorites among the many religious groups in the United States is to ensure a strict separation between them and the government and its public policies. It is especially important, in this view, that public policies do not use tax dollars to fund religious activities. For government to be evenhanded among the many religious groups, it should treat them all the same—by not encouraging, aiding, or recognizing any of them.

Thus strict separationist groups such as Americans United for the Separation of Church and State and the American Civil Liberties Union (ACLU) oppose nativity scenes at Christmastime and other religious displays on public lands, the reference to God in the Pledge of Allegiance, organized prayers or the questioning of evolution in public schools, and government funding of religious schools. They opposed the funding of the evangelical student publication at the University of Virginia and the display of the Ten Commandments mentioned at the beginning of the chapter.

What could be simpler? Or more just? If government is not to show any favoritism to any one religion, government should have as little as possible to do with religion. Strictly separate religion and government and government's evenhandedness will be assured. But will it?

The problem is that public policies such as this would not be evenhanded between religious groups and activities, on the one hand, and thoroughly secular, nonreligious groups and activities, on the other. An example will help.

Milford is a small town of three thousand residents in central New York State. Stephen and Darleen Fournier, Milford residents, asked permission to start a Good News Club for elementary school children that would meet in the school after normal school hours, as did other social, civic, and recreational groups. Parents would have to give written permission for their children to attend. Meetings would consist of prayer, Bible stories, memorizing Bible verses, and snacks.

The Fourniers were turned down by the school authorities, because their proposed Good News Club meetings were religious in nature. Government, in effect, would be helping to spread religious beliefs. Thus began a long court battle.

The Supreme Court decided in 2001 that the school district was in the wrong and the Good News Club must be allowed to use the school's facilities. The Court ruled that to do otherwise would be to discriminate against religion. Explaining the Supreme Court's decision, Justice Clarence Thomas wrote that "there is no logical difference in kind between the invocation of Christianity by the Club and the invocation of teamwork, loyalty, or patriotism by other associations to provide a foundation for their lessons."[4] Evenhandedness meant that an organization using Christianity to encourage moral development should be treated the same as a secular organization using "teamwork, loyalty, or patriotism" to encourage moral development. To allow the secular organizations to use the school facilities and to deny Christian organizations to do so would discriminate against religion.

If only secular groups may use school facilities, and if in countless other ways public policies may support and recognize only secular organizations and viewpoints, religion and its organizations and viewpoints would be discriminated against. Government would then no longer be evenhanded or neutral between the religious and the secular but would be tilting in favor of the secular. This is not justice.

Those who urge the strict separationist approach make an unexamined assumption: that if government sponsors no religious references or symbols and supports no religious activities or organizations, then it has created neutral ground where no one's deepest beliefs are advantaged or disadvantaged. But they could not be more wrong. In today's world, Christian and other religious worldviews are competing with thoroughly secular worldviews. Whether it is called secular humanism, humanism, secularism, or a secular cultural ethos, one is referring to a force in American culture that poses the most formidable competition for the hearts and minds of our neighbors—and of our children.

Thus when, under strict church-state separation, public policies recognize, sponsor, or support nonreligious, secular organizations and their points of view—and not religious ones—government is favoring them over religious organizations and points of view. Government is no longer being neutral or evenhanded. It is clearly supporting one of the sides in the most significant moral, truth-seeking divide in American society today—that between nonreligious, secular worldviews and Christian and other religious worldviews.

There is a better way. It seeks to put legs on the basic principle that just public policies will be evenhanded, or neutral, toward people of all faiths as well as secularists with no religious faith. The equal treatment or neutrality principle argues it is proper for public policies to recognize and support religious organizations, symbols, and practices, as long as it is recognizing and supporting those of the wide variety of religions found in the United States, and as long as it is recognizing and supporting religiously based and secularly based organizations, symbols, and practices alike. In that way religion, including Christianity, is recognized and honored for what it is, but Christianity is not being put into a favored position above other religions or secularism.

> "Banishment of religion does not represent neutrality between religion and secularism; conduct of public institutions without any acknowledgment of religion *is* secularism."[5]
>
> —A. JAMES REICHLEY,
> POLITICAL SCIENCE SCHOLAR

That is why I believe the University of Virginia had it wrong when it denied funds to the Christian student group while giving them to a wide variety of secular groups. Doing so favored secularism over Christianity, as the Supreme Court rightly found. But Judge Moore, as I will explain shortly, was in the wrong when he tried to display the Ten Commandments in the Alabama judicial building—without any recognition of other religious or secular traditions. Doing so would put Christianity and Judaism, whose traditions include the Ten Commandments, in a favored position over followers of other religions and nonbelievers.

I also believe that the Supreme Court got it right in the case of the Fourniers and the Good News Club. It would not be justice for the school to single out the Good News Club and other religious groups and give them the right to use school classrooms while denying their use to secular groups. If this is so, it is equally unjust for it to single out secular groups and allow them to use school classrooms while denying their use to the Fourniers' Good News Club and other religious groups. And this is exactly what the Supreme Court decided. Equal treatment is the key. Following this principle is more just than either (1) favoring secular belief systems over Christian and other religious belief systems, as does the strict separationist approach, or (2) favoring Christianity over other religious or secular belief systems, as does the Christian-nation approach.

How can these perspectives be used to think through and react to the many concrete church-state issues that swirl around us? I cannot begin to consider all of these issues, but let's together consider three of them.

Three Key Issues

Governmental Displays of the Ten Commandments

There are hundreds of displays of the Ten Commandments in government buildings or the land surrounding them—including the Supreme Court building itself. Many see them as a way to recognize the important role the Ten Commandments have played in the development of law and in Western culture more generally. Similarly nativity scenes or Christmas trees at Christmastime and menorahs at the time of Hanukkah are sometimes erected in public places. Some city and state seals contain religious words or symbols. Ought we to see these as innocent, constitutional ways for government to honor religion and the important role it has played in our history? Or do they favor Christianity, Judaism, or religion generally over secular belief systems? Is government being religiously neutral and evenhanded? Is it being just?

The contentiousness of these questions was dramatically revealed in 2005, when the Supreme Court considered two cases dealing with public displays of the Ten Commandments—and ruled in two five-to-four decisions that one was constitutional and one was not!

The display of the Ten Commandments that was held constitutional consisted of a large stone monument that had stood on the grounds of the Texas State Capitol for forty years. It was held constitutional because there were sixteen other monuments on the capitol grounds: ones honoring everything from Texas pioneer women to the Texas cowboy. The Supreme Court held that this display was constitutional because the Ten Commandments display was only one of many different displays. Religion was not being singled out for special honor or recognition.[6]

But in a second Ten Commandments case decided by the Supreme Court the very same day, it held the display to be unconstitutional. This case came out of Kentucky and involved a display of a framed copy of the Ten Commandments in a county courthouse. The Ten Commandments were a part of a larger display, labeled "The Foundations of American Law and Government." Also included were framed copies of the Magna Carta, the Declaration of Independence, the Bill of Rights, the lyrics of the national anthem, the Mayflower Compact, the national motto ("In God We Trust"), the Preamble to the Kentucky Constitution, and a picture of the lady of justice. All were roughly the same size.

Complicating the Kentucky case—and, as it turned out, highly significant for the Supreme Court's decision—was the fact that the Ten Commandments had first been posted alone. Then, under threat of a lawsuit, the county changed the display to include other historical documents with clear religious messages, such as the opening words of the Declaration of Independence and the national motto. The county changed the display to include both religious and nonreligious documents, as described above, only after losing on the lower court level.

Here the Supreme Court held that this posting of the Ten Commandments was unconstitutional. The key was that the county had first put up the Ten Commandments alone and later posted other religious documents that are a part of our heritage, and still later it added some nonreligious documents. As a result the Court ruled that the purpose of the county all along had been to favor religious aspects of our heritage and added documents other than the Ten Commandments only as a cover for their real intent.[7]

The principle the Supreme Court justices were working to apply in both of these cases is clear: Religious documents and symbols such as the Ten Commandments may be displayed in public places, as long as religion is not being elevated to a favored position. I believe the Court was using the right standard.

That is why I believe Judge Moore and his many supporters—including many evangelicals—got it wrong. To single out the Ten Commandments and honor them for their contribution to the development of law favors the Judeo-Christian tradition over other religious and secular streams of thought that have also contributed to the development of our legal traditions.

But that still leaves the question of whether the Supreme Court got it right in *applying* that standard in the two 2005 cases. I personally believe that when the Kentucky county finally displayed several religious and secular documents that had contributed to the development of law it got it right, and that is what should have governed the Supreme Court's decision. Others will disagree.

The Kentucky case clearly teaches that when we Christians seek to introduce our faith into the public realm we need to do so thoughtfully and with due respect for those of other faiths and of none. I fear that sometimes we do so unthinkingly and with a Christian-nation mind-set lurking in the background. Then one easily falls into the error the Supreme Court saw in the Kentucky county: seeking to favor Christianity and then later seeking to cover up its true intent. We ought not to rush in and later figure out if we went about it the right way. Taking the latter path is wrong. We are violating, even if in a minor way, the religious freedom of our non-Christian and nonreligious fellow citizens, and we are setting ourselves up to lose our struggle in the courts. Being salt and light in the public-policy arena requires thought and care, as well as the respect due our fellow citizens.

But there is another issue. Even when we as evangelicals are careful to push for displays of the Ten Commandments or other religious texts or symbols on public land in such a way that no one's religious freedom is harmed, is it worth going to all the work and effort to do so? Here equally sincere and thoughtful Christians may disagree. Some will argue that it is right and proper—and honoring to God—for our government to recognize the role Christianity has played and continues to play on our nation. To strip the public square of all Christian symbols is to imply that Christianity is of no consequence and our Christian heritage of no significance. Meanwhile, all sorts of secular symbols and events are recognized in the public square. The message being sent—subtly and by default, but nonetheless powerfully—is that religion generally, and Christianity in particular, is of no real consequence in history or today's world. This, these Christians argue, is factually inaccurate and puts our Christian faith at a disadvantage.

But other Christians have asked another question: Given the continuing poverty in our nation, millions of AIDS orphans in Africa, vicious Christian persecution around the world, the threat of terrorist attacks, and other dire needs at home and overseas, ought we evangelicals spend our time and efforts working to place and defend religious symbols in public places? Ought that to be our top priority? These people would argue that they are glad William Wilberforce and his fellow evangelicals two hundred years ago spent every effort to stop the slave trade and promote more humane policies toward India, not to erect a cross in Hyde Park!

School Prayer

"Almighty God, we acknowledge our dependence upon Thee, and we beg Thy blessings upon us, our parents, our teachers and our Country." This is a prayer that the New York school authorities had written to be used at the beginning of school days. In 1962 the Supreme Court held it to be an unconstitutional violation of the separation of church and state. A year later it found that reading from the Bible and reciting the Lord's Prayer were equally unconstitutional.

These two decisions unleashed a firestorm of criticism that continues. Many evangelical Christians still feel that school prayer is a defining issue. It came to symbolize a broader secularization process in our public schools.

Most evangelical Christians have taken one of three potential positions on school prayer. Some have opposed and others supported each of these positions. There is no one "Christian" position. One of these positions is to work hard to *reinstate spoken, teacher-led school prayers.* This is usually what is favored by those who argue in favor of "school prayer." But many Christians see problems with this position.

First, they argue, it favors prayer and therefore religious belief over nonreligious, secular beliefs. In practice most prayer probably would be Christian in a very general, broad sense. Those who oppose such prayers believe it is unjust to impose on the children of nonbelievers and of minority religions prayers that are even vaguely Christian. Second, those who oppose spoken, teacher-led prayers in public schools suggest that those Christians who favor them probably assume that, given the religious makeup of their community, the prayers would be "broadly Christian." But what if they lived in, for example, an overwhelmingly Muslim school district—and any public school prayers were likely to be offered to Allah while facing Mecca. It is argued that their enthusiasm for school prayer would suddenly take a nose dive! Yet this is the position into which Christian prayers put our Jewish, Muslim, Hindu, pagan, or unbelieving neighbors.

I personally believe that the biblical principles I presented earlier in this book argue against spoken, teacher-led prayers in the public schools. They would not be just because all people would not be treated equally. The children of nonbelievers and members of minority religions would be put at a disadvantage. The welfare of us as Christians, not the common good, would be advanced—except, of course, in schools where the children from Christian families are in the minority, and then they would be put at a disadvantage, which is also wrong. Our solidarity with our neighbors who are not Christian argues against subjecting their children to organized prayers. And our respect for the family as a God-instituted aspect of civil society means we should respect the religious faiths of those families that are not Christian.

However, I also recognize that those who disagree with me on this position have a legitimate, defensible position. Those who argue in favor of spoken, teacher-led prayers in public schools point out that these would be voluntary prayers. Any parents who did not want their children to take part in these prayers could ask that their children be excused from class for the brief prayer time. No one would be forced to pray, and those who wish to take part in the prayer could do so. But would the children excused from class during the prayers by that very act be put in a difficult position, labeled as being "different" by their classmates and perhaps subjected to teasing? Some have argued yes. Others claim such fears are exaggerated.

Here, as will often be the case in the seven chapters that apply the basic biblical principles, there will be disagreements among equally sincere Christians. That is OK. The truly important thing is that they have carefully thought through their position, are seeking to test and apply biblical principles, and are voicing their positions with civility, acknowledging that their position is not the only legitimate one for a Christian to hold. What is not OK is to disagree based on unconcern, unbiblical notions, and unexamined assumptions—and to claim to hold the only possible position a sincere Christian should take.

There is a second possible answer to the issue of school prayer: *setting aside a time at the beginning of the school day for silent prayer or reflection.* As with the first option, this also has its supporters and detractors. Under this option each student could pray in his or her own way, and nonbelieving students can simply quietly reflect on the coming school day—or even plan their after-school activities.

Those Christians who favor this approach argue that to many students and their families prayer is an important activity, and it should be recognized and honored as such. When all prayer is removed from the schools, these people feel an implicit message is being sent that prayer—and religion more generally—is unnecessary and unimportant, which is the exact opposite of the message many parents want to instill in their children. Other Christians feel that a moment of silence at the beginning of school days is so meaningless that it is not worth working for.

There is a third response to school prayer and the broader question of religion in the public schools. It is to *supplement public school education by Christian clubs and activities during nonschool hours*. Recall Stephen and Darleen Fournier and their Good News Club in Milford, New York. This is an example of dedicated Christian believers who did not try to interject their faith into the school curriculum but worked to provide Christian activities and instruction in the school—as a separate, clearly voluntary activity. There are also many other examples of Christian student-led clubs meeting during, after, or before school hours.

The basic principle here is one of equal treatment or equal access. If secular clubs and groups are allowed to meet on school campuses during nonschool hours, it is clearly unjust and discriminatory for Christian groups—or other religious groups—to be denied access. The courts have not always, but usually, ruled along these lines.

> "To the extent that a religious club is merely one of many different student-initiated voluntary clubs, students should perceive no message of governmental endorsement of religion."[8]
>
> —SANDRA DAY O'CONNOR, SUPREME COURT JUSTICE

Other Christians have concluded that such efforts are inadequate substitutes for Christian elements being woven into the school's curriculum. They have concluded that an informal club or meeting during nonschool hours is no match for hours of instruction stripped of all religious elements during the school day. Those who favor this third approach—even over a moment of silence at the start of school days—point to the fuller presentation of the gospel that can be achieved in this third approach. They also point out the challenges, if not the impossibility, of integrating Christian elements into the school day in a way that treats justly those of other faiths or of no faith.

Educational Vouchers

Many evangelical Christians are convinced that both a moment of silence and supplemental approaches are inadequate. They desire their children to be taught in school in a way that reinforces and complements what they are being taught in their homes and churches. For them, home schooling or distinctively Christian schools are a necessity.

There are also parents who find their children caught in failing public schools, where they are not learning what they need to learn, are not being stimulated to achieve all that they can, and are not even safe from physical assault and the temptation of drugs. Their God-given human potential is being stifled.

On the K-12 level, many parents in either one of these camps are looking to vouchers as an answer. Under such a program the government provides a voucher worth a certain amount of money available to parents for each school-aged child. They can then "spend" that voucher at a private, religiously oriented school or a private, nonreligious school. Milwaukee, Cleveland, Washington, D.C., and Florida have programs that roughly fit this description, although all four of these programs are limited in scope, and the Florida program was recently found by Florida courts to be unconstitutional under the state's constitution. Vouchers could also be used to offset the cost of home schooling one's children.

When voucher funds are used in Christian and other religiously oriented schools, church-state issues arise. Public tax funds are being used to fund schools that often are very explicitly and intentionally religious in nature. The strict separationist position objects to this. Voucher programs are regularly challenged in the courts. In 2002 the Supreme Court found, however, that under the neutrality or equal-treatment standard a voucher program as practiced in Cleveland, Ohio, does not violate the religious freedom language of the First Amendment. The issue remains controversial. Like Florida, other state courts may find voucher programs a violation of state constitutions.

Christians weighing whether or not to support K-12 voucher programs in their states or school districts face several questions. First, there is the basic question of the injustice of forcing children to attend failing schools. Middle-income parents can usually escape failing schools by buying a house in a school district with strong schools, but parents of modest income often find themselves and their children stuck in an uncaring, unsuccessful school district with no means of escape. Vouchers may be their only hope.

Christian parents who conclude they are fighting a losing battle against the perspectives and values taught in their public schools face the prospect of first paying taxes to support the public schools and also having to pay tuition at a Christian school. Or, if they decide to home school their children, they will have to pay for the public schools and then for the books and materials needed for private instruction. In both cases they may rightly feel that without vouchers public policy is deeply unjust.

But there is also the principle of solidarity. Involved, active parents are a key to responsive, successful schools. If those parents who are most concerned with the education of their children are able to pull their children out of the public schools because of the availability of vouchers, are they living up to their obligation to the broader community? The children who will be left in the schools are those whose parents—due to a lack of education, pressures of single-parenthood and a low-wage

"In sum, the [Cleveland] Ohio program is entirely neutral with respect to religion. It provides benefits directly to a wide spectrum of individuals, defined only by financial need and residence in a particular school district. It permits such individuals to exercise genuine choice among options public and private, secular and religious. The program is therefore a program of true private choice. . . . We hold that the program does not offend the Establishment Clause."[9]

—WILLIAM H. REHNQUIST, SUPREME COURT CHIEF JUSTICE

job, or simple disinterest—are the least able or likely to influence the schools for good. And if the children of concerned Christian parents leave the public schools, are not the parents abandoning the schools—and their neighbors—to secular forces that will now have a clear field to exert even more influence? Solidarity says we Christians ought to identify with the needs of our fellow citizens and seek to support them in those needs. Vouchers may make a troubling situation in our public schools even worse and those children who are left in them even more vulnerable to secularizing pressures or bad educational situations.

One thing is certain: Christians who support voucher programs must support them for students attending Muslim, Jewish, and private, secular schools, and not only for students attending Christian schools. As I have stressed throughout this book, Christian involvement in public-policy issues must be aimed at the common good and justice for all, not at a better deal for ourselves.

Conclusion

Why did I choose to consider church-state issues in the first of the seven chapters that apply basic biblical principles to actual policy questions? Because they go to what lies at the heart of our attempts as evangelicals to influence public policies. Are we working merely to defend our own religious freedom? Or are we working to defend the religious freedom of our Jewish and Muslim neighbors as vigorously as we are our own? Are we seeking to secure a favored position for our faith in the public realm? Or are we seeking to secure recognition for our faith that is equal to but not greater than that given other faiths and secular systems of belief? If we get the answers to these questions right, we will be in a position to move on to consider the public-policy issues I will consider in the next six chapters.

Questions for Reflection and Discussion

1. How do you react to the quotation from Supreme Court Justice Potter Stewart on page 99? Do you think he is right to speak

of the Constitution protecting the freedom of religion for non-Christians in terms as strong as he does for Christians? Why or why not?

2. The chapter argues that the strict separationist principle ends up favoring secular views over Christian or other religious views. Explain in your own words how the chapter makes this point. Do you agree or disagree?

3. Do you think it is important for there to be religious displays, such as the Ten Commandments, in public places? Why or why not?

4. Do you favor spoken, teacher-led prayers in public schools? Explain whether or not you think that excusing children whose parents do not want them to take part in such prayers is an adequate safeguard of their freedom.

5. Do you think a moment for silent prayer or reflection at the start of the school day is a good answer to the school-prayer issue? Or is it so meaningless that it's not worth pursuing? Explain.

6. Do you think Christians should pursue vouchers for K-12 education for their families and others, or should they stay in public schools and try to influence them for good? Be able to defend your answer.

7

Life Issues

"Choose Life"

(Deuteronomy 30:19)

MARGARET GREW UP IN A CHRISTIAN HOME and so excelled in her home schooling that she started college when she was only fifteen.[*] The summer between her freshman and sophomore years, while only sixteen, she worked in a McDonald's restaurant. A divorced man in his thirties—I'll call him Tom—came in and struck up a friendship with her. She was not that interested in him, but he was persistent, and she was too young and inexperienced to know how to say no and make it stick. They dated a few times. Tom told her he was in love with her and that he had been praying God would send him someone just like her. Margaret was at a difficult period in her life. She was struggling with depression and eating disorders. She was not close to her parents.

One thing led to another, and Margaret left home to live with Tom. Her outraged parents said she was no longer a part of the family and was to have no contact with them or her brothers and sisters. Tom turned out to be abusive and controlling. He belittled her and controlled her life totally. And then Margaret discovered she was pregnant.

[*]Margaret and Tom are fictitious name, but the events recounted here are true.

Tom insisted that she have an abortion, but Margaret resisted. Tom would scream at her for hours on end and threaten her. Margaret did not know where to turn. Her family had turned their backs on her, and she was living in a new city where she knew no one. She had no friends; she was young, alone, and confused. When Tom took her to an abortion clinic and demanded she have an abortion, she felt she had no recourse. Reluctantly, full of fear, and crying, she had an abortion.

Since then Margaret has experienced God's healing grace. She is reconciled with her family, is counseling other young women contemplating abortion, and is happily married. She and her husband are joyfully expecting their first child.

Another event: In early 2005 the nation was transfixed by the legal, legislative, and media battles surrounding the case of Terri Schiavo. Fifteen years earlier Terri had collapsed in her home from unknown causes. Her heart had stopped. She received emergency treatment from an EMT crew and was rushed to the hospital. She was resuscitated, but she had suffered massive brain damage. Initially Terri's husband Michael and her family hoped that she would respond to medical treatment and recover some or all of her brain functions. But after years of efforts, those hopes proved false. Her doctors declared her to be in a "persistent vegetative state," though some other doctors questioned this conclusion. Terri was not on life support; she could breathe on her own and her heart continued to beat on its own. But she could not eat or drink; a feeding tube provided her nutrition and liquids.

Terri's husband Michael wanted to remove the feeding tube, which would result in Terri's death. He claimed that he had done all he could to bring Terri back and that she had expressed to him her desire not to be kept alive under such conditions. Terri's parents and siblings wanted her to continue to be given food and drink. Even after fifteen years, they had hopes for her recovery. They felt that at times in some minimal ways she responded to them. And as Catholics they believed it was not morally right to cause someone's death by withholding food and liquids.

A long legal struggle ensued. In the end the courts ruled that Michael could have the feeding tube removed. This was done, and thirteen days later Terri died from dehydration and a lack of nourishment.[1]

Both of these events can be considered human tragedies. The world indeed is not as it is supposed to be. Young women become pregnant under excruciating circumstances, without the God-intended support of a loving husband and a caring family. Diseases or accidents strike and leave people barely hanging on to life and incapable of interacting with their families. Modern medical technology sometimes keeps people from dying but fails to restore them to health.

What should be our response to these human tragedies? What public policies ought government to pursue? What should be left to individual choice? Where—and in what manner—ought government to intervene to outlaw, to mandate, or to regulate?

Let no one pretend these are easy questions with easy answers. If we are to act in solidarity with those in need, we cannot help but weep with those who face a pregnancy under awful circumstances. Or with those who face incredibly hard decisions about the medical treatment for a family member they love more than life itself. These are tough issues, and one should never approach them with a cavalier attitude that does not reach out in love and compassion to those facing enormously difficult situations.

But there are biblically based answers even to difficult questions. Our Lord has not left us without guidance. The biblical principles I discussed in the earlier chapters—creation, justice, solidarity, and civil society—can serve as guides as we think through and react to the personal and public-policy challenges posed by awesome dilemmas of life and death. In this chapter I consider how these principles apply in two areas: abortion and end-of-life decisions.

Abortion

I first ran for public office in 1970. The abortion issue was new to me, as it was to most of the nation. *Roe v. Wade*—the Supreme Court decision legalizing abortion—was still three years in the future. At first I tried—as would any good politician—to find a compromise position that would satisfy both sides. Maybe I could support legalizing abortion in the very early weeks of a pregnancy and outlawing it in later stages; or maybe I could support legalizing abortion only under certain limited, specified conditions.

But as I studied the basic facts of human conception and development, it became clear to me there is no logical, medically valid breaking point where one could say that on one side of the line a fetus is not human life and on the other side it is. From the time of conception—and surely from the time an embryo implants itself in the uterus of the mother—through the stages of fetal development to birth, there is a seamless progression. There is no clear breaking point, as it was once thought, when the mother first feels movement of the developing baby. With medical advances, a fetus can survive outside the womb at ever-earlier stages of pregnancy. Modern science has not been kind to present-day politicians seeking some way to satisfy both the prolife and prochoice sides in this debate!

The Basics

The basic physical facts of human conception and development, as we know them today, show that as soon as a sperm fertilizes an egg, all human chromosomes are present—a unique human life has begun. In about six days, if the process continues normally, the fertilized egg will implant itself in the mother's uterus. There follows an amazing explosion of growth. In a little over twenty days, when the mother first suspects she is pregnant, the tiny embryo's heart has started to beat and its blood to circulate. After six weeks brain waves can be detected. By the twelfth week, the pregnant mother is carrying in a physiological sense a very small, but complete, human being. All of the human organs are present. He or she now only has to grow, gain strength, and fully develop functioning organs.[2]

In a medical, physical sense, there is no doubt that when an abortion is performed a human life is ended. Or—more bluntly—a baby is killed. Our consideration of abortion must begin with that inconvenient fact. If the developing

"In the first fifty days of pregnancy, that tiny ball of cells will change to a little person. . . . The heart, liver, brain, bones, and blood are packaged in arms, legs, head, and trunk. The heart beats and the limbs move. Signals zing along nerves and two eyes are set in a childlike face. These first fifty days hold the most incredible physical transformation of our lives. . . ."[3]

—CHRISTOPHER VAUGHAN, BIOMEDICAL EDITOR AT CAMBRIDGE UNIVERSITY PRESS fetus were merely an extension of the mother's body, as some pro-choice advocates have claimed, there would be one organism—the mother—with two different DNAs. This is a physical impossibility.

Modern science tells us that the developing fetus is indeed a small human being; it does not tell us what importance we should attach to that human being. For that we need to turn to the Bible. And the Bible's testimony is clear. "So God created man in his own image, // in the image of God he created him; // male and female he created them" (Gen. 1:27). As we have noted at many points in this book, human life is precious in God's sight, and therefore it must be precious in our sight.

If justice means anything—if assuring that all people receive what is their due means anything—it means that their right to life itself is protected. Without life we are deprived of everything else that is due us as God's image bearers—freedom to worship God, opportunities to develop our gifts and talents, freedom to marry and raise children, and on and on.

This means a woman's decision whether or not to have an abortion ought never to be a purely personal, private decision. She is choosing not only for herself, but also for someone else. One side of this debate refers to a "woman's right to choose" and labels itself as being prochoice. Our society has rightly decided, however, that there are many things we as individuals do not have as a right of choice: whether or not to dispose of highly toxic chemicals in an unsafe manner, whether or not to take personal vengeance on someone who has stolen from us, even whether or not to play ear-splitting music at 1 a.m. in a quiet residential neighborhood. These actions are not simply matters of individual choice. Why? Because they affect others. They interfere with the health, safety, or convenience of others. The same principle applies to a woman contemplating ending a pregnancy by way of an abortion.

But this only begins our thinking about abortion and public policy; it does not end it. True, justice demands that the life of the unborn child be protected. But what about those women who face difficult pregnancies? Their lives and well-being are also precious in God's sight. They too deserve justice. Recall Margaret, whose story I related at the start of this chapter. She faced pregnancy under incredibly difficult circumstances.

This leads directly to a question that must not be avoided by those—including myself—who insist that justice means that abortions should be allowed only under the most extreme circumstances: What ought public policies do to assist women and their unborn and born children? Surely we as a society have a responsibility, in various and meaningful ways, to assist women who are bearing children under enormously difficult circumstances. Our solidarity with them and their unborn children, as well as their already born children, demands this. But this still leaves many questions.

Public-Policy Issues

Ought all abortions under all circumstances be legally banned? Exactly how much and what type of assistance ought society to provide by way of government and its public policies? What assistance ought we as individual Christians, churches, and nonprofit agencies provide? Three public-policy issues especially demand consideration.

Should all abortions under all circumstances be illegal? One question that divides even many Christian groups is whether or not all abortions under all circumstances should be illegal. Some Christians answer this question with a resounding yes. They cite the medical facts, as I just did, to demonstrate that a developing fetus is indeed a separate, distinct human being. He or she is a person God has created in his image. Killing that person is unjustifiable. Government, in its justice-promoting role and out of solidarity with the most vulnerable of all human beings—unborn children—has a duty always to protect the child.

Others argue that although "no abortions" is the general rule, public policy should allow for a few, limited exceptions. The one most frequently cited is to save the life of the mother. These people argue that if the choice is between the unborn child's life or the mother's life, it is permissible to choose the mother's life. Surely, they argue, this awesome decision is one the family should make with the help of competent medical personnel. Government ought not to impose a uniform policy on all.

Some who would allow abortion under very limited, extreme circumstances also cite pregnancies resulting from rape or incest. Those who take this position usually emphasize that almost nothing illustrates more clearly the broken, sinful nature of this world than a child who has come into existence by a brutal rape or an incestuous relationship. If anything is not as it is supposed to be, it is that of a woman pregnant due to the brutal violence of a rape or of a twelve-year-old impregnated by her own stepfather. Under such horrific circumstances, so the argument goes, there is no good answer. At such times we may need to recognize that in a sinful world, public policies must take into account the depths of the depravity to which human actions sometimes sink. One can conclude that under those circumstances it is not just to demand that the young girl or the rape victim give birth to the child. Solidarity with the unborn child and solidarity with the victim of rape or incest clash. Ought public policies insist that what is due the developing child always outweighs what is due the victim of rape or incest?

Here we need to make an important distinction—between what we as Christians believe should guide our own behavior and what we believe our government's public policies ought to prohibit or legalize for everyone. I know an evangelical Christian who believes that if his own daughter or someone else close to him became pregnant due to rape, he would counsel her against an abortion. He would offer all the support—physical and emotional—that he could give and for which he could arrange. He is sure his whole church would give what help it could. But he is still opposed to public policies that would forbid all abortions under such circumstances. He would counsel a "choose life" decision, but he also believes that, under a situation as wrenching as this, justice does not require public policy to demand this decision—as he feels it should in almost all other instances of abortion. One can agree or disagree with this person, but the distinction between what one personally is convinced is morally right and what public policy should impose on all of society is an appropriate distinction.

Some Christians also argue that there may be a few other, very limited, circumstances when public policies ought not to forbid abortions—as in the case of severe deformities in an unborn child that make survival very unlikely.

Other Christians, however, are convinced that public policies should never allow abortion. In the case of allowing abortions to save the life of the mother, they argue that rarely, if ever, is there a certain, stark choice between the mother's life or the unborn child's life. Thanks to modern medical practices, there is usually a chance— perhaps even a good chance—that the lives of both can be preserved. This exception, they believe, too easily serves as a loophole that will allow abortions even when the risk to the mother is minimal.

Others would make saving the life of the mother the only exception. They insist that even in cases of rape or incest there is a purely innocent party involved—the unborn child. As brutal as rape is and as repulsive as incest is, one ought never to take the life of the innocent party. If justice means anything, these people argue, it means the most innocent of all the people involved in these tragedies is not the one who should pay with his or her life. Because ending the life of the unborn child is at stake, solidarity with him or her must trump solidarity with the rape or incest victim, whose life may be repaired through loving support and counseling. And killing a severely deformed unborn child whose chance of survival is almost nil is no different from killing a person suffering from a terminal illness. Only God gives life, and only God may take it. Public policy must never allow the purposeful, deliberate taking of another's life.

To what extent and in what forms should public policies provide help to women experiencing crisis pregnancies? A second public-policy issue is how we as Christians and as a society ought to provide help to the Margarets of this world. Margaret "chose" abortion, because she could see no other viable solution, given the extreme pressures she was under. We can blame Margaret for succumbing to these pressures, but perhaps we Christians share some of the blame for not providing the support that she desperately needed. I suspect that many women who now opt for abortions would choose to bear their children, if they knew about viable alternatives and assistance that are available.

Thus an important question to ask is whether the needs of women experiencing crisis pregnancies in one's community are being met— and whether information on alternatives to abortion is readily available. If counseling and help are available from one or more crisis pregnancy centers, from churches, and perhaps from government agencies such as local welfare offices, then the only need may be to support and encourage them in what they are already doing.

If such services are not available in one's community, one needs to ask how best to correct this situation. Perhaps a crisis pregnancy center is needed, if none is now present. Perhaps existing agencies need more money from individuals and churches—or from the government.

But what role should government play in meeting the needs of women experiencing crisis pregnancies? Here the civil-society organizations and the principle of subsidiarity discussed in chapter 5 are helpful. They suggest we should first look not to government, but to civil society and its many organizations to provide the help needed. In the case of crisis pregnancies, emotional support usually needs to accompany material, financial help. And government agencies are not where one would normally look for emotional support. But government is often needed as well. It can offer financial assistance to women's resource centers to help them as they provide alternatives-to-abortion information and assist women experiencing crisis pregnancies.

"Recently, I made the choice to terminate an unplanned pregnancy. I thought it was my only option. Afterwards, I found myself unable to cope with what I had done."[4]

—JACQUI, A WOMAN HELPED
BY THE LOS ANGELES WESTSIDE
PREGNANCY RESOURCE CENTER

Today many childless couples long to complete their families by adopting children. And many pregnant women who feel they cannot raise a child are seeking abortions, because they see no other viable alternative. This sad situation can be alleviated by public policies making adoption an easier and quicker process. This should include public policies that allow interracial adoptions—something some states now discourage or even forbid. We are all God's children. Race should not matter.

To what extent and in what forms should public policies provide help to needy mothers who choose birth over abortion? A third public-policy question deals with help for mothers who have chosen life over abortion but are mired in poverty or face other struggles as they care for one or more children. Solidarity with such families and a basic sense of justice requires Christian citizens to support efforts to help these women and their children. Of this we can be confident. But exactly what form that help should take and how best to provide it are prudential questions to be considered thoughtfully and prayerfully. I can offer no neat formula that will supply automatic answers.

Two observations, however, may help. First, government help and assistance sometimes have to play a role. Providing cash assistance, help with housing, and job training and preparation are expensive. Private, nonprofit groups can rarely totally provide such programs, so government-sponsored programs, such as WIC (Women, Infants, and Children), which provides good, nutritious food for needy pregnant women and their children, and TANF (Temporary Assistance for Needy Families), are needed. To oppose abortion and to fail to support public policies that provide programs such as these is not an option for a Christian citizen seeking to be truly and consistently prolife.

It seems to me that both conservatives and liberals are often highly inconsistent. Most conservatives work to protect the lives of unborn children, but then they turn around and work to cut assistance programs for low-income families in need of financial and medical assistance for those very same children after they are born. Meanwhile, most liberals are equally inconsistent. They are unwilling even to protect the lives of unborn children, but once babies are born they are ready to support a range of assistance programs. A Christian approach seeks to defend and protect human life both before and after birth.

A second observation invokes the principle of subsidiarity and holds that often the best assistance government can give is not by programs directly run by government agencies themselves. Instead, government should help finance existing nonprofit agencies—many but not all of which are Christian in character—that are already helping families in need. Then government programs, instead of undercutting existing programs, will strengthen and reinforce the work they are already doing. Local civil-society agencies are often more people-friendly than governmental agencies.

Exactly how these observations translate into concrete public policies is open to question. Much depends on specific circumstances. What I believe is *not* open to question is the duty of Christian citizens to seek out and support both governmental and private, nonprofit programs of help to mothers in severe need who have not resorted to abortion.

End-of-Life Decisions

As medical technology advances, end-of-life quandaries become more, not less, frequent. People who earlier would have died from disease or injuries are now kept alive. The case of Terri Schiavo, cited at the beginning of this chapter, would not have arisen prior to modern medical technology.

As with abortion, Christian principles such as creation, justice, solidarity, and civil society all speak to end-of-life questions. Creation says human life is of immense importance. Justice says governments have the God-given duty to protect and honor human life. And we Christians are called to act in solidarity with those suffering from illnesses and disabilities that strip people of human dignity and cause untold suffering. Civil society and its agencies can play a role in meeting needs associated with end-of-life situations.

A Christian perspective on end-of-life issues also insists that, especially for the Christian, death is not the end, but the beginning. There are worse things than death. Our Savior has removed the sting of death. For the Christian it is a translation into a far better, far more real existence than we can ever know on earth. The apostle Paul expressed well the dilemma many Christians down through the centuries have felt: "I am torn between the two: I desire to depart and be with Christ, which is better by far; but it is more necessary for you that I remain in the body" (Phil. 1:23–24). We are not to hasten or bring on our own deaths, nor are we to fight against death as though we have no hope of a future life.

All this does not yet give us answers to specific situations. To apply these basic principles it is helpful to note that there are three separate end-of-life issues that raise public-policy questions.

Assisted Suicide

One public-policy issue is assisted suicide or euthanasia. In 1994 Oregon voters enacted a physician-assisted suicide law that allows doctors to prescribe lethal doses of drugs. Between 1998 and 2005, 246 persons died under the terms of this law. Compassion and Choices, formerly called End-of-Life Choices and before that the Hemlock Society, is an organization actively pushing assisted-suicide legislation in additional states.

A biblical understanding of human life insists that assisted suicide is never right and should be strictly illegal. We do not love our neighbor as ourselves by wishing or causing his or her death. It is unjust for the government to allow health professionals to take active steps to hasten another human being's death. I cannot think of an argument based on biblical principles that would justify the government's allowing a physician or anyone else to cause another person's death—or more frankly, but equally accurately, to kill another person—even in the face of difficult, debilitating injury or illness.

But this is different from saying that public policies must insist that all active steps must always be taken to prolong a person's life. Just as euthanasia goes against God's will by causing the death of a person whose life is not yet over, so also employing all the latest medical technology to prolong the life of a person who is clearly dying can be seen as going against God's will. This leads to a second public-policy question.

What Level of Care Ought to Be Given to Individuals Who Are Severely Ill or Injured?

On the morning of January 18, 1989, Don Piper was a robust, healthy, thirty-eight-year-old husband, father, and pastor. Life was good. Then just before noon he suffered a shattering auto accident. He was pronounced dead at the scene and experienced heaven in a glorious encounter. But his work on earth was not yet done. In answer to the fervent prayer of a pastor who happened upon the accident, a pulse returned, and Don was rushed off to a Houston hospital. With multiple traumas and fractures, Don began a long, excruciatingly painful process of recovery. In his book *90 Minutes in Heaven,* Don relates how at many times in this process he did not want the medical torture to continue. He wanted to die and experience the joys of heaven. Many people, facing debilitating illnesses or accidents, have felt exactly as Don Piper felt. Death is seen as a welcome friend.

Piper's true story sets the stage for a second key issue or question: What level of care should severely ill or injured people receive? And the follow-up question: What role ought public policies play in legally requiring or assuring the level of care that is in keeping with biblical principles?

As I think about these questions, I find two basic distinctions helpful: (1) between "extraordinary, heroic" measures to prolong a person's life and what is considered normal, standard medical care and treatment; and (2) between medical care—whether heroic or standard—that holds promise of restoring a person to a reasonable measure of health and medical care that is doing no more than dragging out the dying process, with no realistic hope of the patient ever experiencing a basic level of good health and living a productive life.

"I believe, however, that because I faced an unknown outcome and the pain never let up, I kept feeling I had little future to look forward to. Most of the time I didn't want to live. . . . I wanted to be free from my miserable existence and die."[5]

—DON PIPER,
PASTOR, AUTHOR, AND LECTURER

Even though these two distinctions do not lead to clearly recognizable positions I can outline, they help distinguish individuals who lean in one of two different directions. Some have a high standard of extraordinary, heroic measures and hold out hope for recovery even when evidence suggests there is very little hope. Those who lean in this direction argue that only God gives life and only God should take it.

Others have a lower standard of extraordinary, heroic measures and conclude more quickly that there is no hope for recovery. Christians who lean in this direction argue that the preservation of human life is not something to be hung onto at all costs. They believe there comes a time when we need to submit simply and prayerfully to God's will and accept what we wish were not the case. We need to let go of a loved one and commend him or her to God's loving care.

But what does all this have to do with government and public policy? After all, end-of-life decisions are usually made outside the realm of public policy, as family members, health-care professionals, and sometimes a trusted pastor together decide on the appropriate level of care. One way government becomes involved is when family members disagree on the appropriate level of care. Then the courts are often called upon. Some family members wish to withdraw forms of care they consider to be excessive and offering no hope of recovery; others insist that care be continued. This was the case in the Terri Schiavo case, where Terri's husband disagreed with other family members on whether to continue providing her with food and liquids by way of a feeding tube.

When cases relating to end-of-life decisions end up in the courts, Christians who define extraordinary, heroic care by a high standard and who are slow to give up on seeing hope of recovery tend to urge the courts to support highly aggressive medical care. They understandably are convinced that, as God's instrument for justice in society, government should err on the side of protecting life. But Christian principles can also be cited to support less than highly aggressive care of severely ill individuals. Justice is not always on the side of prolonging life. Solidarity with suffering, dying people and their families who are being put through wrenching experiences can be cited as a reason for the courts to favor those urging less than highly aggressive treatments.

This entire topic of the level of care that should be given individuals who are severely ill or injured is one in which equally sincere Christians may disagree as they apply biblical principles. Some will hold to higher standards for extraordinary, heroic care than do others; some will more quickly conclude that there is no hope of restored health. As a result, some will more quickly conclude that the courts should intervene to order continued care than will other Christians. Such disagreements are OK. The important thing is that we rest our arguments on biblical principles, which we sincerely and prayerfully apply to concrete situations.

Providing Support and Help to the Ill and Disabled and Their Families

Diane Coleman is the president of Not Dead Yet, an organization of people with disabilities that opposes assisted-suicide laws. She once stated before a congressional committee: "I'm also sick and tired of our allies on this issue . . . who see assisted suicide and euthanasia as violating their principles, but see no contradiction as they slash budgets for the health care we need to survive."[6] She went on to cite two conservative governors who opposed assisted suicide but also attempted to cut Medicaid funding, which includes funding for items such as ventilators and feeding tubes.

Just as with abortion, when we Christians oppose assisted suicide and seek in other ways to protect human life even when severely disabled or in its final stages, we need to be consistent. That means we must favor support for people with severe illness and disabilities, as well as their families. It is easy to stand up for the rights of people with disabilities and illness to receive medical care; it is harder to pony up when the bill to pay for these services comes due.

This is where government and its public policies come into play. Care for people who are severely ill and life-prolonging procedures are usually extremely expensive. They can involve around-the-clock nursing care, high-tech machines, and enormously expensive drugs. Most individuals and families and most nonprofit organizations cannot afford the ongoing care such people need. And for the family caregivers, there is a physical and emotional burden that is more than most of us can bear alone.

Government, with its ability to obtain large sums of money through its taxing powers, is often the only way these huge medical costs can be met. This is one instance where we evangelicals may need to defy the stereotypes and support more, not less, government spending.

As with abortion, civil society and the principle of subsidiarity come into play here. The care and support for people with disabilities and severe illnesses should come, if at all possible, from local, nongovernmental agencies. Public policies usually can best support families and local, nonprofit agencies, not take over for them. A family may be able to care for a member who is disabled, if it receives some in-home nursing assistance or other help. Many communities have nonprofit hospice programs that offer help and support to those with terminal illnesses. They provide support to the family and care for the dying that emphasizes comfort and relief of pain, not heroic efforts to extend life. Financial help from government is sometimes needed to expand and strengthen the work they are doing. There are others ways that local, state, and even the federal government can help families and local agencies—religious and secular—that provide assistance for people with severe illnesses and disabilities. Christians ought to support the government in these efforts.

Conclusion

As I warned at the end of chapter 1, even Christians who agree on basic biblical principles will sometimes reach different conclusions as they apply those principles to specific, concrete public policy questions. Many of us (and I include myself) will at times be uncertain exactly where we should come down on some questions. That has been the case in this chapter as we have reflected on the issues of abortion and end-of-life decisions. I have tried to avoid insisting on one "Christian" position for every public policy question I have examined. There is room for disagreement among us. The important thing is that we base our concrete positions on biblical principles and conscientiously, thoughtfully apply them while seeking wisdom and guidance from our fellow believers—and most importantly, from God.

Questions for Reflection and Discussion

1. Are there any situations in which you believe a pregnant woman or girl should be legally allowed to obtain an abortion? If so, what situations? And how do you justify government allowing someone to take another human being's life?

2. This chapter claims justice and solidarity should lead Christians not only to oppose all or almost all abortions, but also to favor programs of assistance for those facing crisis pregnancies. Do you agree these two positions should be bound together? Do you think government and its public policies should uphold both of these positions equally? Or should they emphasize one more strongly than the other?

3. This chapter contrasts (1) people who tend to have a high standard for defining extraordinary, heroic medical treatments and are slow to see no chance of restoring someone to health with (2) people who tend to have a lower standard for defining extraordinary, heroic medical treatments and are quicker to see no chance of restoring someone to health. In which of these directions do you lean? Why?

4. Based on the Christian understanding of civil society and the principle of subsidiarity, this chapter suggests that care for people who are severely ill should be provided not directly by centralized government agencies, but, when at all possible, by families and local, nonprofit—and perhaps Christian—organizations. In what ways can public policies be crafted to make this more possible?

8

Poverty

"Be Open-Handed toward the Poor and Needy"

(Deuteronomy 15:11)

PATTI IS A FRIEND OF MINE who dropped out of college to marry the man she loved. They soon had two little boys. She was a full-time mom, while her husband worked as a teacher. Theirs was an all-American, even idyllic, family. Or so it seemed. Then suddenly Patti's husband left, moved to another state, and sued for divorce. Patti soon discovered that her husband had left her with back rent owed on their house, as well as other unpaid bills. She had never held a full-time job and, having left college early, had few marketable skills. Her husband made only sporadic child-support payments; because he had moved to a different state, a cumbersome, inefficient child-support system was unable to collect the financial support that was due her and her two little boys.

Patti was at the end of her rope. She struggled to feed her children and faced the very real prospect of being homeless. Not knowing where else to turn, she obtained welfare through the Aid to Families of Dependent Children (now called Temporary Assistance for Needy Families [TANF]). With the help of her caseworker who was willing to bend a few rules, she returned to college, completed her degree, obtained full-time employment, and was able to leave the welfare rolls.

There is much we can learn from Patti's story. Poverty can strike suddenly and through no fault of one's own. Government-sponsored welfare programs can work as intended, providing desperately needed temporary help while someone obtains skills needed to obtain a job and become a self-supporting, contributing member of society.

But not all stories are like Patti's. Some people are poor because they made wrong, sinful choices and are unwilling or unable to work hard to obtain the training that will lead to employment. Still others are poor due to ill health or deeply embedded psychological problems. Their family backgrounds may never have taught them the attitudes and values needed to compete successfully in the world of work.

The Bible repeatedly calls us to be concerned and to offer help to the poor. That much is clear. Exactly how to translate our concern and offers of help into concrete, practical acts is less clear. And when it comes to the public policies of government, what ought they to do and not do? How ought we as Christian citizens apply the biblical principles discussed earlier in this book to the problem of poverty? These are the questions this chapter explores.

Poverty Today

The poor are still very much with us. The United States Census Bureau has judged that a family of three with an annual income of less than about $15,000 is living in poverty. Based on this standard, it estimates that as of 2005 there were 37 million people, or 13 percent of the American population, living in poverty. Of these 37 million people, 13 million were children under eighteen years of age. Poverty varies by racial and ethnic groups. It was almost three times higher among African Americans (25 percent) than among non-Hispanic white Americans (8 percent). Among Hispanic Americans the poverty rate was 22 percent.[1]

To understand poverty and its negative effects, two additional perspectives need to be understood. First, in the United States poverty exists among unparalleled affluence. While 37 million people live in poverty, 20 million households have incomes of over $100,000 a year. The average annual family income in the United States is $63,000. We are an enormously wealthy country, and most of us are blessed with material goods that others cannot even imagine. The combination of great wealth and poverty existing side-by-side in the same country and even in the same communities raises crucial and challenging questions—even while it does not suggest quick, simple answers for the thoughtful Christian seeking God's will.

A second key perspective is that poverty is more than a simple lack of money to buy the necessities of life. It is that. But it is more. A job that pays decent wages not only pays the rent, puts bread on the table, and keeps the lights on, but it also tells people and their families that they are doing useful, worthwhile work that society values. It daily affirms that they are useful individuals who contribute to society and support those who depend on them. In contrast, the unemployed or sporadically employed, along with those employed at such low wages that they cannot support their dependents, receive the daily message—even if falsely—that they are failures. The implication is that they have nothing of real value to contribute to society, and that those who are depending on them are looking to them in vain. How does one go home and tell one's children that there will not be enough food for them that evening? Or as winter approaches, that there will be no warm jackets or Christmas gifts this year?

> "We live in a country rich beyond measure, yet one with unconscionable ghettoes. We live in a country where anyone can make it; yet generation after generation, some families don't."[2]
>
> —JASON DEPARLE, SENIOR WRITER, *NEW YORK TIMES*

Poverty, with its attending physical and psychological consequences, severely limits people in their ability to live the creative, productive lives God intends for all human beings. God intends that all of us—in joy and thankfulness—be able to develop the abilities he has given us, support and care for our families, and contribute to the broader society. All these are aspects of being God's image bearers. They may not be impossible for the poor to accomplish, but they are certainly made difficult.

The Bible Speaks

I have been told that in the Bible there are more than two thousand references to the poor. I have never tried to count them, but both the Old and New Testaments time and time again insist that as believers we *must* be concerned for the poor. It is a requirement. "There will always be poor people in the land. Therefore I command you to be open-handed toward your brothers and toward the poor and needy in your land" (Deut. 15:11). "Religion that God our Father accepts as pure and faultless is this: to look after orphans and widows in their distress and to keep oneself from being polluted by the world" (James 1:27). I could fill the rest of this chapter, in fact the rest of this book, with biblical commands to care for the poor and needy. Of all people, we evangelicals—who take the Word of God authoritatively and seek to pattern our lives after it—should take these repeated commands seriously. If we ignore them, we deny the authority of Scripture. There is no way to escape this conclusion.

"Our band of eager young first-year seminary students did a thorough study to find *every* verse in the Bible that dealt with the poor. . . . We found *several thousand* verses in the Bible on the poor and God's response to injustice. . . . [Then] one member of our group took an old Bible and a new pair of scissors and began the long process of cutting out every single biblical text about the poor. . . .

When the zealous seminarian was done with all his editorial cuts, that old Bible would hardly hold together, it was so sliced up. It was literally falling apart in our hands."[3]

—JIM WALLIS,
PASTOR AND POLITICAL ACTIVIST

Here the Christian principle of solidarity, discussed earlier, and the many biblical supports for it come front and center. The poor are not somehow "others," separate from us and with no ties of mutual responsibility. They are our brothers and sisters; we are to see Christ in them.

While studying welfare-to-work programs in Dallas, I once interviewed the assistant director of a deeply Christian program that was working with the homeless. She described the philosophy of her agency in these words: "We are faith-based—we strive to be the hands of Christ for the homeless. Our desire is to touch them as if they are Christ himself." Her agency had not only read but was living out Matthew 25:40: "Truly I tell you, whatever you did for one of the least of these brothers and sisters of mine, you did for me" (TNIV). This is solidarity with the poor. Our Lord demands nothing less from us.

Clearly we should live in solidarity with the poor; our attitude must be one of concern, not indifference. But this is the beginning of our consideration of the Christian's duty toward the poor, not the end. How are we to live out this concern in the twenty-first century, in a modern, urbanized society such as ours? And what roles ought individual Christians, nonprofit agencies, and the public policies of government play? The rest of the chapter seeks to give some guidance in answering these questions. Careful thinking and important distinctions are needed.

> "Is not this the kind of fasting
>   I have chosen: . . . ?
> Is it not to share your food
>   with the hungry
>   and to provide
> the poor wanderer with shelter—
> when you see the naked,
>   to clothe him,
>   and not to turn away from
> your own flesh and blood?"
>
> —ISAIAH, OLD TESTAMENT PROPHET
> (ISA. 58:6–7)

The Causes of Poverty

I vividly recall one day back when I was active in Michigan politics and attended a picnic put on by the United Auto Workers for its members. I met a man who had worked for an auto supply firm that specialized in making chrome-plated bumpers for large Lincoln Continentals. His layoff was due to a dwindling demand for these bumpers. He looked thoroughly depressed and plaintively asked me when I thought the economy would pick up, so he would be called back to work. I mumbled

> "Suppose a brother or sister is without clothes and daily food. If one of you says to them, 'Go in peace; keep warm and well fed,' but does nothing about their physical needs, what good is it? In the same way, faith by itself, if it is not accompanied by action, is dead."
>
> —JAMES, APOSTLE AND BROTHER OF JESUS (JAMES 2:15–17 TNIV)

something about not knowing but certainly hoping it would be soon. What I could not bring myself to tell him was that deep in my heart I suspected he would never be called back. He was caught in two trends: a movement to obtain cheaper car parts from overseas and a style change away from chrome-plated bumpers.

We need to recognize that many are poor or threatened with poverty because of forces they cannot control. The man I met at the United Auto Workers picnic was affected by forces that were not of his making. As in the case of my friend Patti, noted earlier in this chapter, women may find themselves with young children and no husband or father in the house due to unfaithful, irresponsible husbands. Or incapacitating illnesses or accidents can strike a family, leaving it with huge debts and no one able to work.

But honesty also forces me to acknowledge that poverty is often due to certain self-defeating actions and decisions. Numbers tell a powerful story. Of all American families headed by a married couple, only 5 percent live below the poverty line. Of those headed by a man without a wife, 13 percent live below the poverty line; of those headed by a woman without a husband, the number jumps to 29 percent. Of those who have not completed high school, 24 percent live in poverty, while of those who have completed high school, even without any college, the number drops to 11 percent. These numbers demonstrate that certain patterns of behavior often lie at the root of poverty.[4] In the United States today, one who completes high school, does not have a child out of wedlock, marries, and remains married is very unlikely to be poor.

I hesitated to write the previous sentence because there is a danger I will be misunderstood. But honesty compelled me to write it. The fact is that many who are poor in the United States today are poor because of their own self-defeating, sometimes sinful choices.

Many people—including many evangelicals—use this basic fact to conclude that the poor suffer poverty due to their own short-comings. Thus they have no responsibility to help them. The old slogan, "I fight poverty, I work," sums up this attitude. It implies that if only the poor would exercise some gumption and get out and work, they would no longer be poor. Surely the Bible doesn't demand that we be concerned for those who are poor due to their dropping out of high school, having children out of wedlock, using drugs, lacking ambition, or engaging in other forms of irresponsible, sinful behavior, does it? They are only reaping what they have sown.

Admittedly, many are poor because of sinful or ill-advised choices they have made. They may have been sexually promiscuous. They may have dabbled with illicit drugs or shoplifted and have a criminal record. Or they may have given up and left high school when things became difficult.

"There but for the grace of God, go I," however is the appropriate response. Who of us is to say that, given different circumstances, a different family situation, a different neighborhood, or a different set of friends, we might not have made the same choices? Our God is a forgiving God, whose grace can cover the worst sins. People who have acknowledged they did wrong, are now trying to make up for past mistakes, and are seeking to do what is right deserve our support and help. Even people who out of discouragement left high school or who out of anger and frustration have given up on trying to find a job and to move ahead are still image bearers of almighty God. If we—perhaps through a tough, demanding love—can encourage and challenge them to become the productive people God desires of all his image bearers, we are indeed doing God's work. We are truly modeling our Savior who has done as much for all of us.

It is also important to recall that in today's world any woman who bears a child outside of marriage had another decision she could have made: She could have aborted that child. Every unmarried mother—even though she made a wrong choice about sex outside of marriage—made the right choice in choosing life over abortion. Surely—as I wrote in the previous chapter—we who as Christians oppose abortion ought to be standing first in line to offer help to those girls and women who chose life; we ought to support public policies that will offer them help.

In the face of poverty, what response does the Bible demand of us? Concern and proffered help. But this does not yet tell us *how* we are to respond. This is what I consider in the next two sections. First, we will look at some basic insights that can guide us as we seek to live out a truly biblical concern for the poor and needy among us. Then we will consider some more concrete applications of those principles.

The Bible, Poverty, and Public Policy: Insights

In the 1960s President Lyndon B. Johnson declared a War on Poverty and, as some commentators put it at the time, "Poverty won." They had a point. Poverty rates barely budged. Discouragement quickly set in.

How ought we as Christians to react? Does our faith speak to what public policies our government should pursue in relation to the 37 million of our fellow Americans living in poverty today? What guidance can the Bible give us as we seek to work against the destructive forces of poverty? There are no simple answers to these questions. The Old Testament Israelites were given many detailed instructions concerning the poor. But theirs was a rural, tribal society, and we live in a largely urban, industrial society that is shifting into a knowledge-based society. We cannot in wooden fashion apply the specific instructions given by God to the Israelites to our society today. But from the principles we considered in earlier chapters, we can uncover some basic insights to apply in our efforts to respond to the needs of the poor among us.

Government Is a Partial, but Not a Complete Answer

Some people think government is the complete answer to the problem of poverty; others think government is never the answer. Both are wrong . . . and both are right. This is a case where a response rooted in Scripture leads us to a both-and, not an either-or, response. While the political right has not looked to government for help quickly enough, the political left has too quickly looked to government for help. It is wrong for Christians who seek to respond to the Bible's call to care for the poor to shove off all responsibility onto government—or to ignore government as a God-instituted means to obtain greater justice for the poor.

There is much that we as individuals and as members of our churches and of a variety of nongovernmental agencies can—and should—do to help the poor. As I will explain shortly, I have stood in awe of dedicated Christian saints who minister to the homeless, the drug-dependent, the poor, the incarcerated, and others of the least of these who live in great need. In doing so, they are ministering to Jesus Christ himself.

However, government and its public policies also have a role to play in alleviating poverty. Often individual and other private efforts to help the poor, as important as they are, can have only a limited impact on poverty. We live in an urbanized, industrialized society—which also means we live in an interdependent society. Indeed, with globalization we live in an interdependent world. People lose their jobs when a manufacturer moves its factory overseas to take advantage of cheaper labor costs. Interest rates go up, and suddenly what had been a struggle to make house payments or keep up with credit-card debt becomes a seemingly impossible task. Or individuals suddenly learn the pensions for which they had worked for more

> "Lord, we know that you'll be comin' through this line today. So help us to treat you well."[5]
>
> —PRAYER OF A FOOD-LINE VOLUNTEER

than thirty years are no longer available due to the bankruptcy of their company. We no longer live on largely self-sufficient farms where we could grow most of our own food and spin and sew most of our own clothes. We live in an interdependent world. This means we are vulnerable. We all need government to protect us from economic adversities that can come with interdependence.

In addition, with its taxing powers, government has money available that dwarfs that of individuals and all but a few nongovernmental agencies. When seeking to help 37 million people living in poverty and millions more living on the edge of poverty, government often is the only institution with the financial resources to make a difference in millions of lives.

Also, sometimes public policies themselves have added to the problem of poverty. Policies may encourage out-of-wedlock births, fail effectively to enforce fathers' support payments for their children, or encourage easy divorce. When public policies are a part of the problem, changing those policies must be a part of the solution.

Antipoverty Programs as Justice

The consistent call of the Bible is that the poor be treated with justice—not that money simply be taken from those with more and given to those with less. As seen in chapter 3, justice can best be defined in terms of giving all people their due. the poor are not treated justly, government is not fulfilling its God-given task. All people deserve an opportunity through work to provide for themselves and their families, to honor their Creator, and to develop and use their gifts and abilities. This is their due. When people wish to contribute to society and support themselves and their families by working but no work is available, or when even full-time wages are so low that they cannot be self-supporting, then justice is not being done.

In a just society, public policies ought to protect the poor from those who would prey upon them and take advantage of them. One thinks of unscrupulous landlords who charge exorbitant rents for dilapidated housing that is as unsafe as it is depressing—simply because the poor have no other choice or have little bargaining power.

But justice also requires that public policies designed to help the poor ought not to degenerate into paternalism, where one person is made so dependent on another that he or she is no longer the willing, contributing, creative person God intends all of his image bearers to be. To give help to the poor without any expectation that they live up to their responsibilities is not the biblical way. It is not just.

In Leviticus 19:9–10 and 23:22, God commanded the Israelites not to harvest their fields to the very edge or to go through their vineyards a second time to pick all the grapes. Instead, they were to leave for the poor the grain on the edges of their fields and any grapes remaining after their first harvest. There are two principles we can gain from this. First, we must, in solidarity with the poor, make provision for them, so that they too can live. Second, the poor have a responsibility to help themselves. The command was not to give a portion of one's harvest to the poor. No, the poor needed to go out in the fields and work hard to glean that which had been left for them.

Similarly both our private actions and public policies should aim to help the poor, but those efforts should normally aim to enable the poor to provide for themselves, not to give handouts with no corresponding responsibilities. Justice speaks the language of opportunities and empowerment. It knows little of handouts with no corresponding responsibilities.

Using Civil Society's Organizations

Several years ago I conducted a thorough study of welfare-to-work programs in four large cities. What started out as an academic research project ended up touching me deeply. I met many dedicated Christians who had given up more promising careers to offer help to the most needy: the homeless, the school dropouts, the unmarried mothers, the drug abusers, and those simply caught up in the confusing competition for gainful employment. I interviewed a young man who had left seminary to work among homeless men in Chicago, for an evangelical agency. I asked him what motivated him to do this work. He responded simply, "God has called me to do this work; this is what I'm supposed to be doing." Then he added that his work also gave him joy: "But there are also challenging aspects of the job I enjoy. These are good folks; they will be good employees. I enjoy working with them."

I also interviewed several people to whom the Christian agencies had offered help. They often recognized the Christian motivations of the staff and volunteers. One said, "It was a Christian program; it was encouraging. It helped get me back on my feet and on the right track. It helped turn me into the mature woman that I am now. They helped a lot." Another testified: "They behaved like Christ. They were gentle, kind, giving, did not discriminate. They gave me a mentor; they taught me spiritually." I repeatedly found myself standing in awe of present-day saints who were doing God's work among the poor and dispossessed of our society.

This brings us straight back to civil society and the principle of subsidiarity first discussed in chapter 5. Public policies ought never to undercut or displace the work being done by civil-society organizations: community-based, nonprofit, and faith-based programs working to help the poor. Public policies should recognize and build upon the work they are already doing. Often the most effective approach for government to take is to work in partnership with local agencies that make up civil society, offering them referrals, financial help, and other supports.

The Bible, Poverty, and Public Policy: Applications

At many points in this book I have stressed that applying even clear biblical principles to concrete situations is a challenge. This is also the case in combating poverty. Even so, in this section I consider two concrete areas as examples of how we can think through specific poverty-related issues in light of biblical principles.

Working for a Stable, Jobs-Producing Economy

The most effective antipoverty public policies may very well be those aimed at creating a healthy, jobs-producing economy. Often people do not see such policies as being "antipoverty" at all. It is true that such policies—when effective—provide economic opportunities and even wealth for the middle class and the affluent. But they also lift many households out of poverty and prevent many people on the economic fringes from sinking into poverty. During the 1990s, generally marked by high employment and low inflation, many people were able to move out of poverty. From 1994 to 2000 the percentage of households under the poverty line dropped from 15 percent to 11 percent. This means there were 7 million fewer people living in poverty in 2000 than in 1993.[6]

But what public policies lead to economic prosperity? Here one quickly gets into very technical, complex issues of taxes, spending, and interest rates that only a bureaucrat at the Federal Reserve Board can love! This is not the place to delve into them. Most of us will always have a difficult time fully understanding them and applying our Christian principles to them.

But one thing is clear: These technical, esoteric issues and the economic results that flow from them are vitally important to the opportunities and challenges the poor face. When we as Christian citizens evaluate the president, Congress, and other national leaders and when we decide how to cast our votes, we ought to ask ourselves how well our leaders are handling the national economy. And we should not first of all ask how well we personally are doing economically. Rather, we should ask how well the economy is doing in offering greater economic opportunities to those near the bottom of the ladder.

Welfare

When it comes to antipoverty public policies, the most frequently debated topic is cash welfare payments to the poor. Many, including many evangelicals, have harshly criticized them. Here again we need to do some clear thinking.

The major program in this category today is Temporary Assistance for Needy Families (TANF), enacted by the federal government. TANF seeks to provide cash assistance to families (usually, but not always, mothers with children) that are economically destitute. Most of the money comes from the federal government, which the states supplement with their own funds. State governments administer the program and set its standards and practices. Thus they vary from one state to another. The TANF program also has certain work and training requirements designed to move those receiving its benefits to full-time employment. In this effort the program provides some supportive help, such as provisions for transportation to jobs and child care. There is a lifetime five-year (or less in some states) limit on being able to receive TANF benefits.

This program continues to be controversial. Some are convinced that the cash payments are too low to maintain families with even minimal necessities, that the five-year time limit is arbitrary and harsh for those who simply cannot find employment, that supportive child care and transportation services are inadequate, and that the training programs are often poorly run and do not lead to jobs. These advocates want higher payments and more work-training programs with generous child-care and transportation provisions. Others, however, are convinced that the program wastes money on people who manipulate the system to avoid work and encourages out-of-wedlock births. They work to cut the levels of cash payments, impose stricter qualifications for help, and compel all recipients to take part in work and training programs. They think a five-year limit on help is too long, encouraging an unhealthy dependency.

Where ought we as Christians to come down in this debate? As I've said, our Lord requires us to show mercy and offer help to those in need. This would lead us to offer more generous help to those in need. But our faith also speaks to a sense of responsibility and of there being consequences for the moral choices we make. Thus some Christians fear that more financial assistance with fewer time limits or work requirements may reward and encourage irresponsible behavior—and, in comparison, penalize those who come from equally trying circumstances but stayed in school, avoided premarital sex, and other ways acted responsibly.

As with many specific, concrete public-policy issues, there is no one obviously Christian answer. Almost all rightly agree that government sometimes needs to provide financial assistance to the poor. When it does so, there are, from a Christian perspective, two important considerations. As we saw earlier, justice should be at the heart of government's efforts to help the poor. This means it should do all it can to avoid creating an unhealthy dependence and rewarding ongoing self-defeating behavior. Instead, it should aim to enable the poor to support themselves through gainful employment.

Thus the welfare system—when it is working within the bounds set by Christian principles—is a two-way street of fulfilled obligations. Society has an obligation to help and support those who are in desperate need. Justice and solidarity demand this. The help given, however, should not consist simply of financial handouts; this creates a dependency and encourages a passivity that undercuts what God has created us to be. The help should enable the poor to overcome the challenges they face, obtain the training and employment they need, and avoid self-defeating attitudes and behavior. But the street runs both ways. The poor who receive help also have obligations. They have an obligation to take advantage of the offered training. They need to work to change the patterns of behavior and the attitudes that are holding them back. They need to accept employment that is offered, even when it is far from an ideal job.

Public policy should insist on this sort of mutual, complementary obligation. To offer help to the poor without expecting anything from them in return is wrong. But it is equally wrong to expect the poor to strengthen their behaviors, attitudes, and work skills without offering them desperately needed assistance.

Does this mean that public policy should offer the poor a year of work-skills training or limit such training to only six weeks? Should the poor be limited to five years of assistance or should it be only three years—or should it be for unlimited years as long as there are needs? When considering such questions, equally sincere Christians searching the Bible and their God-directed consciences with equal fervor may draw somewhat different conclusions. The important thing is that all Christians act out of a genuine, heartfelt solidarity with the poor, seeking their good as God's image bearers with something to contribute to society. We ought not simply look for a way to save on taxes or to feel superior because we are not like "one of them."

A second important consideration for Christian citizens to keep in mind as they seek conscientiously to influence welfare policies is to work with and build upon civil-society institutions. Government policies ought not to undercut or take over for entities that are already working to help the poor. Instead, government ought to affirm, help, and strengthen them in their efforts. This means, first of all, that welfare policies should do all they can to encourage and strengthen stable, two-parent families. Stable, faithful marriages are one of the best antipoverty devices available, as demonstrated by the numbers I cited earlier in this chapter. Public policies that appropriately encourage such marriages and discourage divorce and out-of-wedlock births are effective weapons in efforts to overcome poverty.

One also needs to appreciate the value of nonfinancial assistance—working toward changed attitudes and patterns of behavior, working out difficult child-care or transportation problems, or convincing people that they are individuals of value and with something important to offer to their children and to society. Government agencies are not very good at offering this sort of assistance, while Christian agencies are.

The importance of civil society and the principle of subsidiarity suggest that government ought to turn to Christian and other faith-based and nonprofit agencies to provide much of the actual, hands-on service to the poor. Many are already doing a fine job. The greatest need often is to support and strengthen them in their efforts—and surely not to try to take over for them.

Conclusion

"Be open-handed toward the poor and needy." I chose this phrase from Deuteronomy 15:11 as the subtitle of this chapter. I have not tried to present neat, simple answers that define exactly what this command means for us today. But Scripture and the principles it teaches—when combined with what we know about poverty in the United States today—set down guideposts that point to answers. Through careful thinking, discussion with fellow believers, and much prayer we can find answers that will honor this charge our Lord has given us.

Questions for Reflection and Discussion

1. Do you think Christians in the United States are sufficiently concerned about the poor? Are they obeying the clear commands of Scripture to be concerned for the poor? Or do these commands somehow no longer apply to us today?

2. Many people in the United States are poor because they engaged in wrong, self-defeating behavior at one time in their lives. What do you think this says about our responsibility as Christians to offer assistance to them?

3. This chapter noted that one way the Old Testament law made provision for the poor was not by handouts, but by leaving some crops in the fields for the poor to harvest. What principle underlies this provision? What are some examples of how this principle could be applied in an urbanized, industrialized society such as ours?

4. This chapter argues that when cash assistance is given to the poor, there is a two-way street of responsibility. What are some responsibilities that we as a society owe the poor (either through government or other channels)? What are some responsibilities that the poor who are being helped owe to a society that is helping them?

9

Caring for God's Creation

"The Earth Is the LORD's"

(Psalm 24:1)

IN **2002** A COALITION OF EVANGELICAL ORGANIZATIONS created a stir and attracted nationwide media attention when it launched the What Would Jesus Drive? campaign. Because some cars use more gasoline and take more energy and resources to manufacture than others, some cars affect the creation more negatively than others. Considering this, the group claimed that Jesus indeed cares what type of car we drive.

If Jesus were living physically on earth today, I am not sure what kind of car he would be driving. Maybe, as one comic suggested, it might be a large SUV, so all twelve disciples could ride with him! But I am confident that in selecting a car he would weigh more factors than affordability or intriguing design. He would ask what impact the car would have on his Father's world and the plants and animals he had created. Choosing what car to drive is a moral choice.

But this does not tell us Christians how we ought to think about and react to environmental questions that confront us daily. What are we to think about claims of global warming and steps that are urged to counteract it? What about air and water pollution? Should

147

we indeed all drive small, less-polluting cars, instead of SUVs, as one way to honor our Lord and the earth he created? Should we also take the next step and use public policies to penalize those who drive large, fuel-inefficient cars? These are the issues this chapter considers. I first try to get us onto a solid foundation by suggesting how the basic biblical principles we have been considering apply to questions of the natural environment. Next I consider some unchristian, inappropriate responses to environmental issues that are not in keeping with those biblical principles. Finally I explore three concrete environmental questions facing us as individuals and as a nation today.

"As Christians we confess Jesus Christ as our Savior and Lord. The Lordship of Christ extends throughout every area of our life. Nothing is excluded from his Lordship. This includes our transportation choices. The Risen Lord Jesus is concerned about the kinds of cars we drive because they affect his people and his creation."[1]

—CALL TO ACTION FOR CHRISTIAN LEADERS, "WHAT WOULD JESUS DRIVE?" CAMPAIGN

Creation Care

From Genesis to Revelation, the Bible clearly and repeatedly teaches that God created this world and all that is in it. Genesis 1:1 reads: "In the beginning God created the heavens and the earth." In Revelation 10:6 God's angel "swore by him who . . . created the heavens and all that is in them, the earth and all that is in it, and the sea and all that is in it."

And there is more. God is no watchmaker who, once a watch has been made, hands it over to a purchaser and gives it no further thought. Instead, God continues to claim the earth as his own.

> The earth is the LORD's, and everything in it,
>   the world, and all who live in it;
> For he founded it on the seas
>   and established it upon the waters. (Ps. 24:1–2)

God declared to Job: "Everything under heaven belongs to me" (Job 41:11). And in Psalm 50:12 God insists that "the world is mine, and all that is in it."

In addition, God actively cares for his world and continually maintains it by his will. As the apostle Paul testifies, "For by him all things were created . . . all things were created by him and for him. He is before all things, and *in him all things hold together*" (Col. 1:16–17). The writer of Hebrews makes clear that it was through the Son that God "made the universe" and is still "*sustaining all things* by his powerful word" (Heb. 1:2–3).

There is yet more. God not only sustains what he has created; he takes a joy and a delight in it. Listen to the psalmist's description of the seas:

> There is the sea, vast and spacious,
> teeming with creatures beyond number—
> living things both large and small.
> There the ships go to and fro,
> and the leviathan, which you formed to frolic there.
> (Ps. 104:25–26)

Why did God create the leviathan, a huge sea creature? He made him to frolic in the sea. I once sat on the shore of the Pacific Ocean and saw a pod of dolphins swimming by, gracefully emerging from the water, sailing through the air, and gently settling back into the water. Sometimes they seemed to my untrained eye to be feeding, but other times they seemed to be frolicking for the sheer joy of life. I am sure God takes a very special delight in them.

The only proper response is to stand in awe of what God has created and fall down in worship before him: "How many are your works, O LORD! // In wisdom you made them all; // the earth is full of your creatures" (Ps. 104:24).

We evangelicals rightly reject modern reinterpretations of Scripture that would do away with the historical reality of the virgin birth of Jesus and other miracles to which the Bible witnesses. But I sometimes feel that we do not put the same emphasis on the teaching of Scripture that this earth is not in any real sense ours, but belongs to almighty God, who made it, continues to uphold it, and takes pleasure in it. We, of all people, should accept these as the literal, not some mythical or figurative, truth.

From these biblical teachings, it is clear that we are stewards, or caretakers, of God's creation, not owners who are free to do whatever we please with it. We are placed on this earth for only a brief time. Whatever we possess, we possess only temporarily. As caretakers of things that do not in any final sense belong to us, we are to use, develop, and enrich that which we have been given—including God's world. Remember chapter 2 and the charge God gave to Adam and Eve and, through them, to all of us: "God blessed them and said to them, 'Be fruitful and increase in number; fill the earth and subdue it. Rule over the fish of the sea and the birds of the air and over every living creature that moves on the ground' " (Gen. 1:28). The King James Version refers to humankind having "dominion" over creation.

A steward or caretaker is not someone who exploits and uses up what has been entrusted to his or her care. Adam and Eve were given the task of caring for the garden, improving it, and discovering and developing the riches God had placed there. They were to subdue and rule over it—to have dominion over it. But it was to be a gentle rule that is exercised for the benefit of that which is ruled.

Men and women, as stewards of God's earth, are to care for that earth and its delightful multitude of plants and animals. We are to use, develop, and bring to a rich and full expression what God intends his earth and its plants and creatures to be. We are not to trample and destroy the earth and its creatures in a headlong rush to satisfy our desires.

Here it is also important to recall the fall into sin and the redemption in Jesus Christ, as I discussed them in chapter 2. Because of sin it is all too easy for men and women to abandon their caretaker role to become despoilers and plunderers. Our selfish desires and the urge toward self-gratification are strong and all too easily overwhelm our call to be stewards of what God entrusted to us.

But this is not the end of the story. In Christ Jesus God has redeemed the world and calls us as Christians to act as his agents of redemption. This includes the natural environment. The natural world has been distorted by human sin—"the whole creation has been groaning in the pains of childbirth right up to the present time" (Rom. 8:22)—but the natural world is also included in Christ's redeeming work. He came to set all things right, including human beings' relationship with the creation. As we Christians become faithful caretakers of God's world, we are acting as his agents of redemption.

The biblical principles of justice and solidarity can illumine our work as caretakers of God's creation. We are to care for creation with an eye to others, who are as dependent on the earth and its riches as we are. And the others for whom we should be concerned include our fellow human beings living next door and around the world, as well as generations of human beings yet to come. When my actions so damage the environment that others' health is threatened, when my wasteful use of natural resources makes it harder for others to live full lives, when my actions deprive others of the joy God intended them to receive from the beauties of his world,

> "Only after the fall does 'dominion' become 'dominance,' 'subdue' become 'exploit,' and 'rule over' become 'abuse.' At no time prior to the fall did these terms endow Adam and Eve with the right or power or authority to claim some kind of alien dominance or counterfeit rule. They simply knew nothing else but a godly, grace-filled rule and dominion."[2]
>
> —R. SCOTT RODIN, FORMER PRESIDENT OF PALMER THEOLOGICAL SEMINARY

then I am not acting in keeping with justice and solidarity. I am depriving them of what is due them and am not fulfilling the debt of love I owe them.

Three Unbiblical Views

I have often wondered why my fellow evangelicals often do not show the same zeal in protecting God's creation as they do in opposing abortion or getting prayers back into the public schools. I suspect the answer in part is that many evangelicals have been put off by certain unbiblical positions some environmentalists have taken. Three come to mind.

When I served in the Michigan legislature, there was an environmental group that every two years put out a scorecard of how the legislators had voted on environmental issues they judged to be especially crucial. It usually ranked my voting record very positively. But one year my ranking took a nosedive. I was puzzled; I thought I had been as supportive of environmental issues as I had been in the past. Then I looked at the specific votes that had been used to make up my score, and I understood the problem. This time the environmental group had included a series of votes on the abortion issue, and since I had voted consistently on the prolife side, my environmental score had dropped. I called up one of the leaders of the group and complained—probably more angrily than I should have. He hemmed and hawed a bit, but he ended up saying that many on their board felt that overpopulation was a part of the environmental problem. Without legally available abortions, population growth would not be brought down.

This illustrates one problem many Christians have had with the environmental movement: a belief on the part of some environmentalists that a key solution to environmental problems is to limit or reduce the number of people living on the planet. And abortion is seen as one means needed to gain this end. Many Christians understandably are put off by this position.

The key issue, however, is not simply how many people there are; it goes deeper, involving our lifestyle choices and whether there are public policies protecting the environment. The Netherlands, for example, is one of the most densely populated countries on the earth, yet it does less to degrade the environment than many less densely populated countries due to strong environmental protection laws.

A second viewpoint embraced by some in the environmental movement is that the ideal is a natural world as little touched by human beings as possible. Their desire is to keep the world as pristine and unspoiled by human impact as possible. This too is wrong. God calls us to use, rule over, and develop the natural world. We are to do so carefully, thoughtfully, and lovingly, but the Bible clearly supports our making use of and developing what God has placed in his creation. He has given it to us for our use.

These first two points of view sometimes have led to a third: one that does not distinguish between the Creator and the creation. Some environmentalists so identify humankind, the earth, and the Creator that all three merge into the others. Earth becomes our mother and men and women simply one of many animal species. In its most extreme form, a neo-paganism takes hold, where nature is worshiped and the earth is seen as a living organism. Plants and animals (including human beings) are seen as similar to cells in any other living organism.

But Genesis 1 clearly teaches there were three distinct actors in the creation drama: God the Creator; the universe, earth, and the plants and animals; and human beings. Each is different and distinct.

The existence of unbiblical views among some in the environmental movement, however, is no reason for Christians to ignore the destructive forces affecting the earth today. A biblical understanding of the natural environment and of human beings' relationship to it must avoid the false perspectives of some environmentalists. But someone else's unbiblical viewpoints do not cancel our responsibility to work to protect the creation. In fact, these unbiblical views may have gained so many adherents, because we evangelicals have been too slow to express a carefully thought-through biblical basis for protecting the natural environment.

Three Key Issues

Remember the What Would Jesus Drive? campaign I mentioned at the start of this chapter? Deciding what type of car to buy is indeed a question to which biblical principles speak. This leads directly to the broader question of what lifestyles we as Christians should lead in light of today's environmental concerns. Do we recycle our used materials? At what levels should we set the heating and cooling in our homes and churches? How far do we travel for a vacation? What pesticides do we use on our lawns? All of these decisions, and many more, affect God's creation; all are moral issues to which biblical principles apply.

But there is a problem here. My lifestyle decisions, while they have an impact on God's creation, by themselves have such a small impact that they can hardly be measured. Unless my neighbors—indeed, our whole society and even other societies around the globe—make the same creation-friendly decisions, what I as an individual do appears pointless. This way of thinking has been called the tragedy of the commons. Let's say a village has a common pasture on which all the villagers are free to graze their cattle. It makes economic sense for each villager individually to increase the number of cattle he or she grazes on the commons. But the commons can, of course, only support a limited number of cattle. Thus at some point, as the villagers increase their herds, the commons will no longer be able to support all the cattle—in fact, it no longer will support any cattle at all as the grass will have been destroyed.

The natural environment is like the commons. The air we breathe, the water in our oceans and streams, the fish in the seas, the myriad of plants and animals in tropical rain forests, the minerals in the earth, and more are available to all. No one person's use of them has a measurable impact. So it makes a certain sense, from the point of view of an individual, to make use of these resources without calculating one's actions' effects on others. But as we all do this, we are in danger of destroying the commons—the environment on which we all depend.

That is why governments and the public policies they formulate are so important. True, changes in our individual lifestyles are also important: They witness to our neighbors what it means for us as Christians to faithfully care for God's creation, and they are a part of a consistent life of gratitude to Christ Jesus and all he has done for us. But more is needed. Recall William Wilberforce. He lived a personal life fully and consistently dedicated to his Savior. Never in a million years would he himself have owned slaves or invested his money in the slave trade. But he also recognized his duty went further. If he was to stop the slave trade and other evils of his day, he needed to act politically. Today if we are to stop the ongoing abuse and destruction of God's creation—if we are to be faithful stewards of God's earth—we must also work to influence the public policies of our nation.

Here I examine three of today's key environmental issues: the extinction of many species, air and water pollution, and global warming. In all three areas our individual actions are important; our actions as citizens who support certain public policies are, in some respects, even more important. Again, I hope to make concrete the application of the principles I have laid out.

The Extinction of Species

The numbers are depressing. The World Conservation Union estimates that more than fifteen thousand species of plants and animals face a risk of extinction in the near future. This includes one in four mammal species, one in eight bird species, and one in four conifers (or what are usually called evergreen trees and shrubs). About one thousand species become extinct every year.[3] As one evangelical theologian, Steven Bouma-Prediger, has written: "Three species every day. Every eight hours another species gone forever. Given . . . that only one to ten species become extinct each year due to natural causes, the conclusion is inescapable: We are experiencing a 'human-caused biotic holocaust.' "[4]

The major cause of this frightful situation is the loss of habitat on which animals and plant life depend for survival. As forests are cut down, urban areas expanded, or lands ripped up for mining minerals, many species can no longer survive. Other major causes are overexploitation of some species by hunting or fishing and the pollution of certain species' habitats.

If we evangelicals truly believe that God created, upholds, and takes delight in his creatures, the loss of thousands of his creatures due to human actions should be a major concern. Human beings are destroying what God has created.

There are things we as individual Christians can do: not buy products made of exotic wood that comes from tropical rain forests; support organizations, such as the Nature Conservancy that purchases for preservation habitats important for the survival of certain species.

As is often the case in protecting God's creation, however, governments and their public policies are indispensable. The United States has an Endangered Species Act. Christians should be in the forefront of pushing for its vigorous enforcement. Our country should support international agreements such as the Convention on Migratory Species and the Convention of International Trade in Endangered Species of Wild Fauna and Flora. Christians should be leading voices in supporting initiatives such as these.

"Consider a recent study saying thousands of animal species, including polar bears and hippos, are in danger of extinction. Logically, an evolutionist should not care: According to his worldview, species come and go, with the fittest surviving to evolve to a higher plane. But a Christian would believe that God created each of these species. Therefore, their existence is His will."[5]

—GENE EDWARD VEITH, CULTURE EDITOR, *WORLD* MAGAZINE

But we must also recognize that we sometimes face hard choices, choices that will divide equally sincere Christians. An example may help. Throughout the 1990s in the Pacific Northwest, a controversy raged around the spotted owl, a threatened species that lives in the old-growth forests of Oregon and Washington. Large segments of old-growth forests were declared off-limits for logging in an attempt to save the spotted owl by protecting its habitat. But this meant many in the timber industry lost their jobs. Men and women who wished to support themselves and provide for their families by useful, gainful work in the timber industry could no longer do so. In Washington State alone, thirty thousand forest jobs were lost.[6] God created and cares for the spotted owl; he also created men and women and smiles when they do good, honest work to provide for themselves and their families.

What side of a controversy such as this ought Christians to support? Christians will have a high view of an animal, such as the spotted owl, that God created and has given to our care as stewards of his creation. But, as I noted earlier, Christians will also resist equating human beings—God's image bearers—with an animal species. We should attach great importance to men, women, and children and their ability to provide for themselves and to contribute to their communities through the development of their God-given gifts.

There will often be answers to such dilemmas that do not require us to choose one side or the other. We should diligently search for such answers. Perhaps new jobs through education and retraining can be found for those thrown out of work due to protecting the habitat of an endangered species. Perhaps new, suitable habitat can be found for endangered species in areas where there would not be negative economic consequences. But such alternatives sometimes prove impractical, or at best they usually require additional time and expense. Often we as a society find it easier to let the endangered species die off or let the people thrown out of work shift for themselves.

Or what of a third-world country that wishes to cut down a tropical rain forest to expand agricultural production? More of God's creatures will be driven to extinction, but many extremely poor citizens of that country will have economic opportunities they have not known before. We in North America turned vast forests and prairies into cities and farmland in our process of economic development. Are we now to try to stop third-world countries from doing the same for their citizens? Does not our call to act in solidarity with the world's poor mean we should put their welfare ahead even of the extinction of some plant or animal species?

We ought never to assume that protecting the creation and its creatures is a simple task. There will be trade-offs, and Christians will sometimes disagree in specific situations over what should be done. I believe we should err on the side of protecting the species God has created. But that is not the same as insisting that protecting species from extinction ought always to trump all other values. Surely, in working to protect plants and animals from extinction, we should take into account and seek to lessen the costs that will fall on some people. We must approach such issues with thought, humility, and a deeply felt concern for all who will be affected by our decisions—plants, animals, and human beings.

Air and Water Pollution

The 2000 film *Erin Brockovich* is based on a true story of how Pacific Gas & Electric (PG&E) was improperly disposing of toxic chemicals near the hardscrabble desert town of Hinkley, California. As a result, toxins were seeping into the groundwater, and there was an unusually high incidence of cancer and other diseases. Erin Brockovich, played by Julia Roberts, was a single mother of three and a paralegal who took on the powerful PG&E. Through persistence and sometimes brazen tactics, she won a settlement for the town's residents.

This film gives a moving example of a second key environmental issue: air and water pollution. This issue is more than a question of blue skies and pristine waters to enjoy while on vacation. Americans are dying because of our fouling of the air and water. The Web site of the California Air Resources Board describes in matter-of-fact, bureaucratic language the life-and-death stakes in pollution: "Health effects from elevated concentrations of PM [soot-like particles] include increased respiratory diseases, lung damage, cancer, and increased mortality. Health effects from elevated concentrations of O3 [ozone] include breathing problems, lung tissue damage, and premature mortality. Elevated levels of toxic compounds may lead to chronic health problems such as cancer."[7]

God made his creation a safe and good home for the human race and others of his creatures. It cannot be his will that men, women, and children—his image bearers—suffer premature deaths due to our using the air and water as dumping grounds. Nor can it be his will that fish, birds, and other animals suffer death due to humans' fouling their homes with our refuse.

What is to be done? How ought we as God's appointed caretakers of his creation act in the face of air and water pollution?

There are things we as individual Christians can and should do to combat air and water pollution. We need to be aware of how our actions contribute to the problem. The manufactured products we buy, the plane trips we take, the electricity we use, the gas and oil with which we heat our homes, the car trips we take all add to air and water pollution. As the comic-strip character Pogo put it: "We have met the enemy and he is us." As we make thousands of consumer decisions each day, we need to weigh the effect of these decisions on air and water. Living more modestly, using up and re-cycling what we have, and using more energy-efficient products are ways to honor the Creator.

But government and the public policies our federal, state, and local governments enact play a larger role than our personal choices as individuals. Only through joint action can we as a society move ahead in cleaning the air we breathe and our groundwater, streams, lakes, and oceans. The Clean Water Acts of 1970 and 1972, as well as the Clean Air Act of 1967, which was strengthened in 1970 and again in 1990, have had positive impacts. Lakes and streams are cleaner than they were forty years ago. Today Los Angeles has fewer days in which it is out of compliance with federal air-quality standards than it did thirty or forty years ago, even though its population and the number of cars have increased many times.[8] Yet more efforts are needed.

But governmental actions to stop the pollution of air and water are not without controversy. In 2004 Governor Arnold Schwarzenegger of California vetoed a bill that would have required California ports to hold constant the large amounts of pollutants being put into the air by diesel-burning ships, trains, and trucks that operate at California ports. He claimed if he had signed the bill into law, it would have cost shippers too much money and, since it only applied to California ports, driven them to ports in other states.

As is the case in this example, public policies designed to protect the environment often involve economic trade-offs. We can clean the water and air, but—as economists like to say—there is no free lunch. A bill will come due in the form of higher prices for the goods we buy and sometimes higher taxes to pay for the increased regulation. One cannot say what the correct, most Christlike, justice-promoting answer will be in all circumstances. But the sincere Christian, who takes the Bible seriously when it proclaims God as the Creator of a good earth and us as his caretakers of it, should weigh heavily the value of a cleaner, healthier earth for all his creatures—and for us to pass on to our children. Usually—even if not always—cleaner air and water should take precedence over economic concerns.

Global Climate Change

Is the world getting warmer? If it is, is this due to human activities or is this a variation in global temperature similar to what the earth has seen before? What will be the consequences of the earth warming? And can we, in any case, do anything about it?

Some things are clear. The earth is getting warmer—about 1.4 degrees Fahrenheit in the past one hundred years. No one disputes this. Nor that there is a much higher concentration of carbon dioxide in the earth's atmosphere now than at the beginning of the industrial age around 1750—from about 280 parts per million to 381 parts per million today, an increase of about 35 percent. There is also agreement that the increase in carbon dioxide is largely due to the burning of fossil fuel: coal, oil, and gas.[9]

But from here disagreements start to emerge. Is the warming that has been measured due to the increase in carbon dioxide? There is persuasive evidence to support this case. Almost all scientists agree that carbon dioxide along with other gases and water vapor act as greenhouse gases, or a blanket, preventing the sun's heat from reflecting off the earth and escaping out into space. As the amount of carbon dioxide in the atmosphere increases, it stands to reason that the earth will become warmer.

More questions arise, however, when it comes to the issues of how much and how rapidly the earth will become warmer and with what effects. We can project future increases in carbon dioxide levels in the atmosphere. But one can always challenge the assumptions on which projections are based. Also, there may not always be a one-to-one relationship between carbon dioxide in the atmosphere and a rise in the earth's temperature. Because 70 percent of the earth's surface is covered with water, and because water heats very slowly, there is a time lag of ten to twenty years between factors that cause global warming and observable effects. All this introduces elements of uncertainty. The best estimates are that the earth will warm another two to nine degrees Fahrenheit during the twenty-first century. Compared to earlier periods of Earth's warming, this increase will happen at breakneck speed.

More questions arise concerning the effects of global warming. Sea levels are certain to rise due to melting ice caps and because warmer water expands. But estimates of how much they will rise vary. Some predict swings in rainfall patterns, with some areas receiving violent deluges of rain and others experiencing droughts. Hurricanes and typhoons may become more violent. Europe may actually become colder, if changes in the earth's climate weaken the Gulf Stream, which now carries warm water from the tropics toward Europe.

Although the exact consequences of changes in the earth's climate are unknown, there clearly will be major consequences for the earth and its peoples, plants, and animals. And they will occur rapidly. There will not be generations for people and animals to adapt and change. The process of species extinction noted earlier will likely increase dramatically. As many as 150 million people may be displaced as they flee low-lying areas that will be covered with seawater. And it will be the poor—especially those living in the developing countries of Africa, Asia, and Latin America—that will have the most difficult time adjusting to these changes. Many do not have the resources to move to new areas or to protect themselves. Even though we do not know the exact consequences of global climate change, we do know that change is coming and that it will have major consequences.

This means global climate change must be a concern for all Christians. Our role as Christ's agents of redemption in a broken world and the principles of solidarity and justice demand no less. What concrete form that concern should translate into, however, is a more difficult question.

As with the other environmental issues discussed in this chapter, we need to consider both personal and public-policy changes. Anything we can do to change our personal lifestyles so that we use less fossil fuel is helpful. We are again back to more-fuel-efficient cars. (We do need to ask what Jesus would drive!) More reliance on carpools and public transit are options; walking or bicycling instead of driving may be practical for some. We can conserve energy in heating and cooling our houses and churches.

But governmental action is essential. Many Christians understandably believe public policies should be changed to require more-fuel-efficient cars and to encourage the use of renewable energy sources such as wind power and solar. Generating electricity by nuclear power is opposed by some Christians, especially given the challenge of safely disposing of waste products that are highly toxic for thousands of years. Others understandably believe that the threat of global warming warrants greater reliance on nuclear power.

International, even global, action is needed. Thus Christian citizens should support our government's entering into international agreements that commit us and other nations to reduce the amount of greenhouse gases, such as carbon dioxide, being put into the atmosphere. We can disagree on the details to be included in these international agreements and whether any specific agreement—such as the Kyoto Treaty rejected by the George W. Bush administration—is the right way to go, but the need for them is clear.

We as American Christians have a special responsibility. Americans make up only about 5 percent of the world population, but we are

> "There is absolutely no question that these [climate] changes will severely threaten life, including human life, on this planet. It would be shamefully ignorant and morally inexcusable if we did not do everything in our power to prevent these changes from occurring."[10]
>
> —ERIC CHIVIAN, M.D., DIRECTOR, CENTER FOR HEALTH AND THE GLOBAL ENVIRONMENT

> "Let me appeal to the Christians of America: take this problem [of global warming] seriously, starting now."[11]
>
> —SIR JOHN HOUGHTON, BRITISH SCIENTIST AND EVANGELICAL CHRISTIAN

putting 20 percent to 35 percent of the greenhouse gases into the atmosphere.[12] Our nation is a big part of the problem. But we can also be a big part of the solution. With our technology and wealth, we can lead the way in finding new energy sources that do not put the same amounts of greenhouse gases into the atmosphere and in finding new ways to reduce the amount of carbon dioxide released when we burn fossil fuels. We may also need to lead the way in helping poorer nations adjust to changing environmental conditions brought about by global climate change. Again, the wealth with which God has blessed us can help.

Conclusion

This last section on global climate change—like the sections on species extinction and air and water pollution—has been long on pointing out general directions, but short on advocating specific steps to be taken. I have done so purposely. Part of the freedom that we in Christ have been given is to work out how God is calling us to live in the specific situations in which he has placed us. The duty to protect and care for God's creation is clear; some basic steps in that direction are clear; some improper responses are also clear. This still leaves much for us as individuals and citizens to weigh prayerfully: What in concrete form is our Creator God asking us to do as caretakers of his creation?

Questions for Reflection and Discussion

1. This chapter suggests that we are stewards or caretakers of God's creation. How does this perspective differ from a typically secular perspective toward the natural environment? In a sentence, try to articulate your personal view of human beings' role in the natural environment.

2. The chapter suggests that making changes in our individual lifestyles will, by themselves, have very little effect on the environment. Do you agree? But does this make such changes

unimportant? What does this say about efforts to influence the environmental policies our government adopts?

3. Do you think endangered species should be protected even if doing so means some people will be thrown out of work? Why or why not?

4. Would you be willing to pay more for the goods you buy or the services you receive, if this is the cost of reducing air and water pollution? Even if it means reducing your standard of living?

5. The consequences of global climate change are not fully known, yet if we wait until they are fully known, it will be too late to do much about them. In light of this uncertainty, what do you think the principles of justice and solidarity say about our duty toward those people who are most likely to be hurt by global climate change?

Violations of Human Rights

"He Has Sent Me to Proclaim Freedom for the Prisoners and . . . to Release the Oppressed"

(J e s u s ,   i n   L u k e   4 : 1 8 ,   q u o t i n g   I s a i a h   6 1 : 1)

IN JUNE 2002 SOON OK LEE, A CHRISTIAN who had been a prisoner in a North Korean prison camp, gave this testimony before the United States Senate Committee on the Judiciary:

> The cast iron factory was considered the most difficult place to work in the entire prison. Christians were usually sent there to work. I was carrying a work order to the cast iron factory in the male prison. Five or six elderly Christians were lined up and forced to deny their Christianity and accept the Juche Ideology of the State [that Kim Jong Il is god]. The selected prisoners all remained silent at the repeated command for conversion. The security officers became furious by this and killed them by pouring molten iron ore on them one by one.[1]

These North Korean prisoners thereby joined the "great cloud of witnesses" honored in Hebrews 11 and 12. They are present-day heroes of faith whose faithfulness to Jesus Christ most of us can only pray we too would show, should we ever find ourselves in a similar situation.

I could fill the rest of this chapter with stories of present-day Christian saints who have been martyred for their faith in Jesus Christ. The numbers are horrendous. It is likely that more Christians were martyred in the twentieth century than in any other century of Christian history. One scholar estimates that as many as 159,000 Christians are martyred for their faith every year—that is an average of more than four hundred Christians killed every day for their faith![2] Paul Marshall estimates 200 to 250 million Christians face persecution for their faith, and another 400 million Christians live under serious restrictions on the practice of their faith.[3]

And Christian persecution—as horrendous as what it is—is only a part of the story of human rights violations around the world. Although it is impossible to come up with firm numbers, there are many non-Christians who also are persecuted and killed for their faith, the Baha'i in Iran, the Falun Gong in China, and other faiths in other lands.

In the Darfur section of the African country of Sudan, hundreds of thousands have been slaughtered by marauding bands of Arab Muslims. Millions have been displaced from their homes. Meanwhile the central Sudanese government has encouraged and backed the marauders. In 2004 President George W. Bush declared this an instance of genocide, and the United Nations has struggled to end the carnage.

> "I have always envied those Christians who all through the church history were martyred for Christ Jesus our Lord. What a privilege to live for our Lord and to die for Him as well."[4]
>
> —MEHDI DIBAJ, AN IRANIAN EVANGELICAL PASTOR IN A LETTER TO HIS SON SHORTLY BEFORE BEING KILLED BY IRANIAN AUTHORITIES

Then there is present-day slavery, dark and evil:

Reena was brought to India from Nepal by her maternal aunt, who forced the 12-year-old girl into a New Delhi brothel shortly after arrival. The brothel owner made her have sex with many clients each day. Reena could not leave because she did not speak Hindi and had no one to whom she could turn. She frequently saw police officers collect money from the brothel owners for every new girl brought in. . . . Reena escaped after two years and now devotes her life to helping other trafficking victims escape.[5]

Estimates of the number of people in the world today being held
as slaves range from a low of 12 million[6] to a high of 27 million.[7]
Either number is horrific. Many are girls who have been forced into
brothels; others are domestic or factory workers who are forcibly held
against their wills and compelled to work without pay—the precise
definition of slavery.

"Slavery is not legal anywhere
but it happens everywhere."[8]

—THE ADVOCACY ORGANIZATION
FREE THE SLAVES

If one needs any proof that
the world is not as it is supposed
to be but is so broken that the
depths of human beings' inhu-
manity toward others can defy
description, one need look no
further than vicious, unrelenting
religious persecution, the horrors of modern-day slavery, and other
denials of basic human rights.

How should we as American Christians react to the depth of evil
revealed by horrendous violations of God-given human rights? As I
have discussed this question with various Christians, I have found that
almost all are appalled at the violations of human rights—and especially
at deadly, bitter religious persecution and slavery—but they also often
feel powerless to do anything about it. How can I do anything about
what is happening in North Korea, India, China, or Iran? All of us are
in danger of stumbling into the trap of despair I discussed in chapter 1.
We can try to influence our American government and urge it to oppose
human rights violations in countries around the globe. But that is itself
a challenging task and still leaves questions of what our government can
do, what it should do, and how it ought to go about doing it.

These are the questions this chapter considers. I first consider
how basic biblical principles can guide our thinking and actions. I
next consider the significant influence evangelical Christians already
have in this area. In the last section I consider four key questions that
frequently arise when seeking to end religious persecution, slavery,
and other human rights abuses in today's world.

Biblical Principles

I challenge anyone to spend even a half hour cruising Web sites
such as those of the Hudson Institute's Center for Religious Free-

dom and Free the Slaves without coming away with a profound feeling that there is no area where the healing, redeeming grace of Jesus Christ is more needed than in the case of religious persecution and present-day slavery. As we saw in chapter 2, through his life, death, and resurrection Christ is redeeming the fallen, broken world. The world Christ came to redeem surely includes the horrific worlds of torture and death being meted out to those who refuse to disown him. It also includes the sordid world of brothels filled with teenage (and younger) girls who have been forced into prostitution against their wills and factories where people work under oppressive conditions against their wills and without pay. We are called to be God's agents of redemption—and that surely includes the horrendous worlds of religious persecution, slavery, and other human rights abuses. As we will shortly see, the evangelical church in the United States is beginning to respond to this call—with positive results.

In thinking through our work as God's agents of redemption in the field of religious persecution and slavery, it is helpful to make a distinction between civil rights and human rights. Civil rights are those that are spelled out and protected by a specific government and its constitution and other laws. They are enforceable in courts of law. Human rights are God-given. They are rooted in all human beings having been created in the image of almighty God himself. As such we are creative, willing, morally responsible beings. The freedom to worship God as we choose, the freedom to express our ideas and beliefs, the freedom to choose our own careers, and in other ways to act as creative, morally responsible beings are inherent in what it means to be God's image bearer. This means all men and women everywhere possess human rights. No government gives us our human rights; no government can take them away. Specific governments sometimes ignore and trample on our human rights, but what God has given no government can take away.

This means that a teenage girl held against her will in a brothel and forced into prostitution, or a Christian believer facing harassment and arrest in China, or a resident of the Darfur region of Sudan who is raped and forced from her home all possess basic human rights. Their rights are being violated, but they are still image bearers of God with all the rights God intends for them.

This leads us to the biblical principle of solidarity. Solidarity with all of God's children—rooted in our obligation to love others as ourselves—demands that we do what we can to stop religious persecution, to stop girls being forced into prostitution, to stop people being enslaved in forced-labor factories, and to stop other blatant violations of God-given human rights. This solidarity surely extends to our brothers and sisters in Christ who are being threatened, imprisoned, tortured, and killed because they are refusing to deny their Lord. We should learn from their devotion and faithfulness, and—in whatever ways we can—stand in solidarity with them. But we also should stand in solidarity with those who are not Christians who are suffering martyrdom for their faith or for other reasons being tortured and enslaved. We are commanded by our Lord to love our neighbors as ourselves, not to love only our neighbors who are also our fellow believers.

Justice is another basic biblical principle that applies with compelling force in the case of religious persecution and modern-day slavery. When the freedom to worship God is denied by way of threats, imprisonment, and torture, or when people are enslaved—forced into prostitution or compelled to work long hours under cruel conditions—a dark, evil injustice is being done them. They are being denied what God intends for all his image bearers. One struggles to find words strong enough to describe the depths of the injustice being carried out.

Having been established by God to oppose injustices and to promote greater justice, governments have a God-given duty to work against religious persecution and for religious freedom for all and to work against slavery and "to release the oppressed," in the words of Jesus quoted in the subtitle of this chapter (Luke 4:18).

But this leaves a question that is not as easy to answer. Most of the religious persecution and most present-day slavery is happening not in the United States, but in other countries around the world. Does the American government have a responsibility to seek to correct the injustices that other governments are carrying out or are allowing within their borders? And do we as American citizens have a duty to try to influence our government to do so?

It is important to begin our discussion by recognizing the enormous power and influence of the United States in today's interdependent world. We are the world's sole superpower. As such we have enormous military, economic, and moral, or persuasive, power. This fact leads to two observations, both of which argue in favor of the United States working actively to end the injustices of religious persecution and enslavement.

First, it is almost impossible for the United States to be neutral toward injustices in which other nations are engaging. If we are not actively opposing them, we will be indirectly supporting them. If, for example, we are not condemning and bringing pressure to bear on a nation that is condoning the trafficking in young girls for the sex trade, we will be aiding that nation in its unjust practice. As we trade with that nation, allow our corporations to invest in it, and engage in diplomacy with it, we will be giving it greater legitimacy and strengthening its economy and government. In a very real sense, if we are not against religious persecution and slavery, we will be supporting these horrendous practices.

A second observation can be illustrated by an example. Let's say you know that a next-door neighbor is abusing a young child. You have observed it; you have seen the bruises; you have heard the screams. But you do nothing about it. "I ought not to be poking my nose into the family affairs of others," is your attitude. Thus you do not alert the proper authorities or speak to your neighbor about it. Would you not be partly responsible for what is going on? I think so.

In the same way, for the United States, with its enormous power and influence, to do nothing when people are forced to work in slave-labor factories, teenagers are abducted and kept against their wills in brothels, and Christian converts are imprisoned, tortured, and killed is wrong. We would become partly responsible for the horrendous acts that are going on.

This still leaves the question of what we as individual Christians ought to do and what we should be asking our government to do. More on that shortly. But indifference and inaction are not in keeping with biblical principles. God is clearly asking more than this from us.

What Is Already Being Done?

Michael Gerson, an evangelical, worked in the White House as President George W. Bush's chief speech writer. He has recounted:

"During my time in the White House, the most intense and urgent evangelical activism I saw did not come on the expected values issues—though abortion and the traditional family weren't ignored—but on genocide, global AIDS and human trafficking. The most common request I received was, 'We need to meet with the president on Sudan'—not on gay marriage."[9] Others have also taken notice of evangelical concern over issues of religious persecution and the trafficking of slaves. Political scientist Allen Hertzke has written: "From the mid-1990s onward born-again Protestants have provided the groundswell for initiatives against religious persecution, trafficking, and other abuses."[10] Another scholar, Walter Russell Mead, has written: "As evangelicals have recently returned to a position of power in U.S. politics, they have . . . given new energy and support to U.S. humanitarian efforts."[11]

Anyone who doubts the ability of evangelicals to have an impact on American public policies needs to look no further than their impact on our nation's laws related to religious persecution and slavery. Evangelicals played a key role in the 1998 passage of the International Religious Freedom Act, which established an Office of International Religious Freedom and a Commission on International Religious Freedom in the State Department. In 2000 evangelical activists and their allies won passage of the Trafficking Victims Protection Act, and in 2002 the Sudan Peace Act. Evangelical members of Congress have played key roles in the passage of such laws.

"Thanks largely to evangelical support (although Catholics and Jews also played a role), Congress passed the International Religious Freedom Act in 1998, establishing an Office of International Religious Freedom in a somewhat skeptical State Department."[12]

—WALTER RUSSELL MEAD,
FELLOW FOR U.S. FOREIGN POLICY,
COUNCIL ON FOREIGN RELATIONS

As a result of these successes, Allen Hertzke reports, "Promotion of religious freedom is now statutorily a 'basic aim' of American foreign policy. The debate now is not *whether* but *how best* to ameliorate the pandemic of global persecution."[13]

But the struggle is not over. When I was elected to the Michigan legislature, one of the first lessons I needed to learn was that the passage of a bill into law was not the end of a process, but the beginning. One of the first (and fairly minor) bills of which I won passage required the Department of Natural Resources to conduct a land-usage inventory. I accepted the congratulations of my colleagues, relaxed, and cast about for other causes to promote. About a year later I discovered that nothing had happened. No land inventory had taken place; none was planned. Bureaucratic resistance, a lack of funds, and other priorities had taken over.

It is almost always this way in the real political world. Passage of a new public policy only means the new policy has been authorized; there is now a legal basis for acting. But those who are charged with carrying out the new policy will often be skeptical of it, have other priorities, and hope that in time everybody will forget about it (so they can carry on as before). All this is to say that concerned citizens and groups need to monitor the new policies enacted by Congress in the past ten years that give new directions to American foreign policy. They will sometimes need to apply public pressure or work to see that Congress appropriates sufficient funding. Christian citizens and their organizations must continue to stay involved and demonstrate their concern. In addition, new legislation may be needed to deal with new problems as they arise or as shortcomings in existing policies emerge.

There is a danger that the attention of Christians will turn elsewhere; as a result, needed funds or the political will may dwindle away and follow-up actions will languish for a lack of interest and support. As long as religious believers are being persecuted, young girls are being sold into prostitution, workers are being forced to work under inhumane conditions without pay, and other human rights abuses are occurring, solidarity and justice require Christians to remain concerned and involved.

Key Issues Today

Throughout much of the 1990s, civil war raged in Sudan, with the Muslim-dominated central government clashing with the largely Christian south. The central government and its allied Muslim extremists often engaged in the capture and enslavement of southern Sudanese, many of whom were Christian believers. Often they were held as slaves for years. One response to this tragic situation was for Americans and Europeans to purchase the freedom of these slaves. A fifth-grade class in Colorado raised some fifty thousand dollars to purchase the freedom of Sudanese slaves. Christian Solidarity International (CSI), a Swiss-based organization, was especially active in these efforts.

What could be more Christlike than freeing the helpless victims of present-day slavery? Yet this practice proved to be highly controversial. It was feared that purchasing the freedom of slaves with money raised in the United States and Europe would only encourage the enslavement of even more people. The slave traders would make "easy money," and with the money purchase more weapons and gain other means to enslave even more people. Was purchasing the freedom of slaves improving or making worse the ongoing tragedy?[14]

As this example illustrates, it is often difficult to develop proper, thoughtful responses to human rights abuses. There are few easy, obvious answers. It is as important for concerned Christians to be "shrewd as snakes" as it is for them to be "innocent as doves" (Matt. 10:16).In this section I consider four specific questions that often arise when appropriate responses to the tragedies of religious persecution and modern-day slavery are debated.

Government or Nongovernment Agencies?

The first question involves *the relative merits of relying on the American government versus relying on the wide variety of Christian and other nonprofit overseas relief and development organizations.* In the evangelical world, organizations such as World Vision, World Relief, and Samaritan's Purse are already active in overseas relief and development activities. These and a host of Christian and non-Christian organizations with similar goals often address issues of religious persecution, sex trafficking, and other human rights abuse. Commonly called NGOs (nongovernmental organizations), they are a part of civil society whose institutions play an important role in God's ordering of society.

This leads to the question of whether we Christians should turn primarily to these NGOs to fight against human rights abuses or rely primarily on our government to deal with them. Government action is not always the most appropriate response, but relying solely on

NGOs is also not always the most appropriate response. The need is to sort out which type of response is most appropriate and when a combination of both governmental and NGO action is best.

Often governments themselves engage in or condone religious persecution, or they look the other way as slavery flourishes. Then some action by the American government will usually be needed: Economic and diplomatic pressures may help, as well as positive inducements, such as offers of trade or economic assistance. Sometimes our government's bringing to light and publicizing human rights abuses can have an impact. In such situations we as Christian citizens need to discuss this issue with our representatives in Congress and in other ways bring the need for our government to take action to the attention of our officials.

But there are situations where NGOs—with or without the support of our government—can take the lead. This often is the case when educational and economic development efforts are the most effective answer to sex trafficking, other forms of slavery, and religious persecution. Human rights abuses can develop or be made more severe when people are without hope for the future and conclude their only way to get ahead is by exploiting their fellow human beings. Those who are being exploited may give up and feel there is no alternative but to accept the trap in which they are caught. In such cases educational and economic development programs may be a better answer than threats and sanctions. And government-to-government assistance often will be less likely to lead to positive results than NGOs directly offering help to local communities. In addition, NGOs can offer help to victims while waiting for governments to work out more basic, continuing solutions. Often the American government can best offer assistance by channeling it through NGOs that are already on the ground in countries with extreme need. Doing so is in keeping with the principle of subsidiarity and supporting, not ignoring or undercutting, organizations that make up civil society.

Governmental Pressure or Dialogue?

When the American government becomes directly involved in addressing human rights abuses, the question often arises *whether to put economic and diplomatic pressure on the offending country or to establish dialogue and create cultural and economic ties.* How, for example, can American policy best work to stop the persecution Christians continue to face in China? Should we strengthen our economic, diplomatic, and cultural ties with China by encouraging young Chinese to study in the United States, having exchange visits of students or businesspeople, opening more consulates in China, encouraging more American investment in China and more Chinese investment in the United States? Those taking this position argue that as ties develop, the Chinese government may become more moderate, and we can informally, gradually influence the government toward greater religious freedom.

"There were multiple viewpoints. One camp believed that you attract a lot more through honey than vinegar, so forget about sanctions. You go to these countries and you say, 'How can I help you promote religious freedom?' You don't wave sticks over their heads. Others said, 'Look, this constructive engagement stuff has proven to be a dismal failure. Let's start leveraging our authority and throw our weight around.'"[15]

—AN UNIDENTIFIED EVANGELICAL LOBBYIST COMMENTING ON THE PASSAGE OF THE 1998 INTERNATIONAL RELIGIOUS FREEDOM ACT

Others believe we should bring pressure to bear on China. We could threaten to cut Chinese imports to the United States unless the government allows greater religious freedom. We could withhold other trade advantages. We could threaten to reduce diplomatic ties and offer more support for an independent Taiwan (bitterly opposed by the mainland Chinese). Those taking this position argue that threats against the self-interest of a country such as China are the only language it is likely to understand. Anything less will be seen as weak and easily ignored.

There is no right answer between these two positions. Both can be effective in some situations and ineffective in others. One cannot say one is more "Christian" than the other. And equally sincere Christians will sometimes disagree on which one ought to be pursued in which situations.

It is important, however, for the wise Christian to note that impure motives can attach themselves to both of these positions. We need to be aware of other people's possible hidden agenda. Sometimes strong business interests oppose cutting trade and cultural ties as a means to stop Christian persecution, sex trafficking, and other evils, not because they genuinely think such efforts will be ineffective, but because their business interests will suffer. Similarly people who favor threatening the cutoff of economic and diplomatic ties may be motivated by a macho swagger and a nationalistic pride that makes them feel good, rather than by a realistic belief that doing so will be effective.

Christians should ask themselves whether either of these traps is lurking unexamined in the back of their minds. They might be influencing the positions they take more than a heartfelt desire for greater justice for the peoples of other lands.

Our Government Alone or a Coalition?

A third issue that frequently arises is *whether the United States can best act alone or act through the United Nations or other large coalitions of nations.* When the United States acts alone, it can act more quickly and decisively but with less "moral authority" than when it acts in concert with other nations. When the United States acts through the United Nations or other international bodies, months and even years may drag on while it works to develop a consensus on the issue. Meanwhile, the killing goes on, sex slaves languish and die in brothels, or people face imprisonment and torture because of their religious beliefs. Here we need, carefully and prayerfully, to balance the urgency to act against the greater authority and greater likelihood of success if we wait and work with other nations.

Military Action or Not?

A fourth issue that sometimes arises is *whether or not American military action—or its threatened use—is called for.* North Korea is probably the most evil regime on the earth at this time. It actively tortures and kills Christians because they refuse to recognize its ruler, Kim Jong Il, as a god, and tens of thousands of its citizens suffer and die from starvation while its rulers live in luxury. There is no freedom. Should the United States threaten to use military force to achieve a change in the regime and unite the north with South Korea, which is democratic, prosperous, peaceful, and Christian to a significant degree?

After the difficulties and lack of progress following our overthrow of the Saddam Hussein regime in Iraq, few Americans—Christian or otherwise—would advocate this path. Neither would I. And yet . . . We must also be careful not to live our comfortable lives of peace and plenty, where our biggest deprivation is not having an HD television set, while our brothers and sisters in Christ are being imprisoned, tortured, and killed. An overly aggressive, we-can-right-all-the-wrongs-of-the-world foreign policy is wrong. But an overly passive foreign policy that ignores our fellow human beings who are grievously hurt and bleeding can also be wrong. At some point some Christians may conclude military action against North Korea or other especially evil regimes can be justified in biblical terms. Fortunately there usually are many options between passively ignoring great evils and using military force in an effort to put a stop to those evils.

Conclusion

Whenever I consider the enormous evils present in human rights violations, the chief lesson I take away is that complacency is not a permissible option for us. There are many areas of the world where people's God-given human rights are being trampled on. As Christians there are things we can do—through our churches, our missionaries, and our overseas relief and development agencies. There are also things we can do as Christian citizens. Our country is probably the most powerful country in the history of the world. It has enormous economic, cultural, and military power that potentially can right some, even if not most and surely not all, human rights abuses. This puts a huge responsibility on us evangelical Christians, who have the potential for much influence on American policies. We should use the God-given influence we have as Christian citizens to move our country's public policies so that they make every effort to stop what human rights abuses they can. Solidarity and justice require no less. They should be our first response.

Questions for Reflection and Discussion

1. How do you feel when you read about Christians being tortured and killed for their faith or about young girls being forced into

prostitution and held against their wills in brothels? Do you identify with the victims and feel pain for them? Or do you find such situations so removed from your everyday experience that you have trouble identifying with the victims? How *should* you feel?

2. Some people believe that the United States ought not—as they put it—to be a moral busybody going all over the world trying to right every wrong we see. We have enough wrongs in our own country that need correcting. Others believe that with the enormous worldwide influence God has given us, we have an obligation to try to right especially serious human rights abuses. Which side do you tend to favor? Which side do you think is more biblical? Why?

3. Do you think the United States should try to correct evils such as religious persecution and sex trafficking by way of persuasion and building contacts with the offending governments, or by the threat and use of economic and diplomatic sanctions? Is one or the other method more biblical?

4. Do you think there can ever be such great evils being carried out by another government that the United States is justified in using military force to put a stop to those evils? If so, what are some situations where you think military force would be justified on biblical grounds?

11

Disease and Poverty in Africa

*"He Heals the Brokenhearted
and Binds up Their Wounds"*

(P s a l m   1 4 7 : 3)

ON MARCH 26, 2005, *New York Times* columnist Nicholas Kristof wrote from the African country of Zimbabwe:

> So with Easter approaching, here I am in the heart of Christendom. That's right—Africa. One of the most important trends reshaping the world is the decline of Christianity in Europe and its rise in Africa and other parts of the developing world. . . . I stopped at a village last Sunday morning here in Zimbabwe—and found not a single person to interview, for everyone had hiked off to church a dozen miles away.[1]

Kristof is right. The twentieth century saw an amazing growth of Christianity in Africa. In 1900 there were about 10 million Christians in Africa; in 2000 there were 360 million. One scholar has estimated that by 2025 there will be 633 million African Christians.[2] More Anglicans attend church on a typical Sunday in Kenya, Uganda, Tanzania, Nigeria, and South Africa —each country separately—than Anglicans and Episcopalians will attend in Britain, Canada, and the United

States combined![3] The explosive growth of Christianity in much of the southern half of the world, and especially in Africa, is an amazing, gratifying, but often unnoticed, story. There is reason to thank God and rejoice at the great work he is doing in Africa today.

But all is not well in Africa. A 2005 official British Commission for Africa began its report with these words: "African poverty and stagnation is the greatest tragedy of our times."[4] The World Bank estimates that more than 40 percent of Africans living south of the Sahara live in poverty.[5] Some 218 million Africans live on less than one dollar a day.[6] HIV/AIDS is ravaging many African countries: "My people are dying. They are dying before their time, leaving behind their children as orphans, and a nation in a continuous state of mourning."[7] These are the words of King Mswati III of Swaziland in a speech before the United Nations General Assembly in 2001. It is estimated there are 26 million Africans infected with the HIV virus. Each year about 2 million Africans die from AIDS. Some 12 million children have been orphaned because their parents have died of AIDS.[8] Less publicized, but also tragic, is the number of deaths each year in Africa from malaria. A staggering 1 million people (800,000 of them children) die each year from this disease. That is one child every thirty seconds![9]

This chapter considers what the response of us as Christian citizens should be to the "greatest tragedy of our times" that is occurring in Africa. We are called to care for the sick and poor whoever they are and wherever they live. The biblical principle of solidarity demands this. We surely should stand in a solidarity of concern and help when the area of the world in greatest need is also the area of the world where millions are turning to a new life in Christ.

It is important to begin with an awareness that Africa is not a poor continent. It is a rich continent with a host of natural resources, good agricultural land, great natural beauty, and an energetic population eager for greater education. God has truly blessed Africa. The question we face in this chapter is what we as American Christians should do—through our churches, our overseas relief and development agencies, and our government—to work with the people of Africa, so they can defeat the evils of poverty and disease and create societies more fully marked by justice and shalom.

In this chapter I first consider how the biblical principles we have been considering in this book relate to the African situation. Next I note that American evangelicals are taking a new interest in the needs of Africa, and then I consider several approaches we can take to help meet the needs of Africa. In the final section I consider what we as Christian citizens can best do to help Africans meet three specific problems: the HIV/AIDS pandemic, the prevalence of malaria, and widespread poverty.

"Africa is suffering not because of scarcity but because what she has is not utilized. God is reminding us that he is ready to liberate Africa from her problems if her people will avail themselves and make use of what he has given them."[10]

—ISAAC NJARAMBA MUTUA, PASTOR, AFRICA INLAND CHURCH OF KENYA

Biblical Principles

The 2006 movie *Blood Diamond* tells the story of civil war that raged for much of the 1990s in Sierra Leone. Tens of thousands died, 2 million people—one-third of the population—fled their homes. Especially horrific was the rebels' practice of arbitrarily amputating by machetes the limbs of those caught in their net and of forcing boys as young as eleven and twelve to fight and kill. As one missionary to Sierra Leone commented, referring to the civil war: "If you don't believe the devil is alive and well in the world, go to a place like Sierra Leone and see the work that he does."[11]

Anyone will have a renewed sense of evil in our world, if he or she even partly understands the terror of random executions and of people being driven off their land, or if he or she has looked into the eyes of a child dying of malaria or has seen a young mother ravaged by AIDS. Shalom at times seems no more than a faint memory. But there is no place so marked by evil that God's redeeming, healing grace does not also reach. In chapter 2 we saw the reality of evil, but we also saw that Jesus Christ and his grace are active in this world—in the Northern Hemisphere and also the Southern. Later we will meet some of God's saints who are his means of grace in Africa today. Hope and a trust in the power of God's grace, not despair, are our proper attitudes toward even the deep troubles that many in Africa are now going through.

Other biblical principles we have discussed throughout this book are also highly relevant to what is happening in Africa. We need to keep in mind that justice is the God-given purpose of governments. Some African governments and their rulers are conscientiously working for greater justice for their people. They are working hard to promote education for all, better health care, and economic development. But other governments are anything but just. Some rulers have squandered money from natural resources on luxuries for themselves and their favored cronies, while many of their people live in poverty and suffer the ravages of HIV/AIDS and other diseases.

What influence the United States has in Africa should be directed at (1) enabling and encouraging governments that are seeking to promote greater justice for their people, and (2) pressuring those governments that are acting unjustly to act with greater justice. At times American policies toward Africa seem to be guided more by what is in our own self-interest than what is just for the peoples of Africa. If an unjust, dictatorial government is willing to assure a steady flow of oil or other resources to the United States, we are tempted to look the other way while that same government treats its people and their needs with indifference. That is wrong.

Solidarity calls us as Christians to stand as one with those who are suffering in Africa. This obligation is strengthened by the large and growing number of Christians in Africa. Out of the eight hundred thousand children dying of malaria each year and out of the 26 million Africans infected with HIV/AIDS, we must remember that many are our brothers and sisters in Christ. One part of Christ's church is suffering; another part is living in affluence. We—the affluent part—are surely called to act. Of that we can be certain.

Civil society, as a God-intended aspect of all societies, and the principle of subsidiarity are also important to keep in mind as we think about the needs of Africa. We have learned by experience that government-to-government assistance is often wasted, as money is siphoned off to support grandiose but impractical programs or to Swiss bank accounts of corrupt officials. Meanwhile churches, as well as faith-based and other nonprofit agencies, are often already operating effectively on the local level. Making use of local, African churches and nonprofit organizations working on the local level—both African and American—often leads to significant accomplishments.

American Evangelicals Begin to Move

"There was a quote box in the middle of the article that read: *'12 million children orphaned in Africa due to AIDS.'* It was as if I fell off the donkey on the Damascus road because I had no clue. I didn't know one single orphan."[12] These are the words Kay Warren—wife of Rick Warren, author of *The Purpose Driven Life*—used to describe her awakening in 2002 to the devastation that AIDS is wreaking in many parts of Africa.

Since then she, her husband, and many others at Saddleback Church, which Rick has pastored, have done much to deal with the AIDS crisis and other needs in Africa. They have toured Africa, raised money, and started a now wide-spread program that links American churches with African churches to work together to deal with dire needs. It is termed the P.E.A.C.E. plan: Planting or Partnering with churches, Equipping servant leaders, Assisting the poor, Caring for the sick, and Educating the next generation.[13]

The Warrens are not alone among evangelicals in living out a deeply felt concern for poverty and disease in Africa. World Vision, an evangelical overseas relief agency, has an HIV/AIDS Hope Initiative that works to stop the spread of HIV/AIDS and bring help to AIDS orphans. Other evangelical relief and development agencies, such as Samaritan's Purse and Feed the Hungry, have similar programs.

Evangelicals' concern has been noticed in the White House. In his 2003 State of the Union address, President George W. Bush announced a new initiative to combat AIDS in Africa and elsewhere, termed the PEPFAR (Presidential Emergency Plan for AIDS Relief). It is making $15 billion available over five years in support of efforts to prevent the spread of AIDS, to care for those already infected, and to provide for those orphaned by AIDS. Twelve of the fifteen countries that have benefited from this initiative are in Africa. Much of this money is being funneled through faith-based organizations, including evangelical agencies. President Bush has also initiated a $1.2 billion effort to combat malaria in Africa.[14]

These initiatives have puzzled some Washington observers. President Bush is known for his conservatism: for cutting taxes and insisting on smaller government, not for new spending programs. But in the case of programs to assist Africa, he advocated and won new spending beyond what the liberal Washington establishment had been urging. In part, the explanation lies in the fact that evangelicals—in and out of government—made a case to Bush administration officials that the American government needs to do more to meet the dire needs of Africa.

Nevertheless, the tragedy of Africa continues to unfold. This raises the question of what more needs to be done. We evangelicals must be compassionate as we seek to be good Samaritans to the people of Africa; we must also use the wisdom God has given us so that we take the most effective approaches to helping Africa. Recall William Wilberforce. He and his fellow Christians acted with compassion as they labored to end the slave trade and enact other reforms, but they also acted strategically. We must do no less.

Helping Africa

When one offers help to another, one must avoid a suffocating paternalism that assumes those being helped can do nothing to help themselves and that the donor knows exactly what needs to be done. To create dependence is to treat others as something less than the image bearers of God. But to ignore the needs of others who are suffering grievously is also wrong.

Any help that we as American Christians offer to Africa—what form should it take? Should we look to our government and its public policies to provide the needed help? Or should we fear intrusive, heavy-handed government programs that can do more harm than good? Maybe we should rely on our churches and Christian overseas relief and development agencies and do our part by supporting them with our prayers and gifts. This section considers three forms that American help to Africa can take.

One form of American assistance is government-to-government aid. Here the American government sends money, loans, or food and other material goods to another government. That government then uses that assistance to help its people. Experience teaches that although government-to-government assistance can and sometimes has achieved much good, often it is not the best way to go. It is easy for foreign governments to use the money for large-scale, showy projects that have more to do with the egos of the rulers than helping ordinary citizens. At worst, the money ends up in the private bank accounts of corrupt rulers and their allies.

This brings us to a second form that assistance to Africa can take. This is assistance given by churches and Christian nonprofit overseas development agencies. I am thinking of agencies such as World Vision, World Relief, Catholic Relief Services, Samaritan's Purse, and many more. Many denominations have their own overseas development agencies. There are also many secular nonprofit development agencies that are doing good work. These private agencies typically have people on the ground, whether Americans or citizens of the country being served. They also often have ties with local churches, health clinics, schools, and social-service agencies. They have networks in place that enable the aid to bypass governments that are sometimes corrupt or simply ineffective.

This approach has advantages over programs of assistance that go through centralized government offices. The assistance is much more likely to reach the people and areas where it is most needed, to support projects with long-term payoffs, and to avoid waste and outright fraud.

But there is also a huge disadvantage to this approach. It is a fact of life that the financial resources of our government dwarf those of private, nonprofit agencies. The United States Agency for International Development (USAID) operates with an annual budget of some $10 billion.[15] As seen earlier, President Bush's five-year PEPFAR program to combat HIV/AIDS is a $15 billion program. His program to combat malaria in fifteen African countries has been allotted $1.2 billion. No church, no private overseas development agency, can come close to matching these numbers.

We should remember that these huge sums represent money we have sent the government in the form of taxes. It is only right for us as Christian citizens to urge our government to use some of our tax dollars to help meet the overwhelming needs in Africa.

But must we choose between supporting often ineffective government-to-government aid programs or Christian and other nonprofit aid programs that are limited by inadequate funds? Happily, there is a third alternative, and one that is in keeping with a strong, vigorous civil society and the principle of subsidiarity. It is for the American government to channel much of the money it has available for assisting African countries through faith-based and other nonprofit overseas development agencies. Individual Christians, churches, and nonprofit agencies are usually not the full answer; nor are American government aid programs. A both-and answer is usually better than an either-or answer.

Dr. Peter Okaalet is a good example of this principle. He is a physician, a pastor, and the African director of the Medical Assistance Program (MAP) International, an American-based Christian relief and development agency. Working through African churches, he has done much to stem the spread of HIV/AIDS and to meet other health needs in several countries. Money MAP has received from the American government has indirectly helped support this effort. This is often the best approach. It shows respect for and builds upon civil-society institutions already in place in African countries, and follows the principle of subsidiarity by relying on local, on-the-ground networks rather than creating more centralized, government-run networks.

> "Churches will always be there. Governments can go in and go out, but the congregations are always there with the people. The church will run a hospital even when there is war."[16]
>
> —PETER OKAALET, PHYSICIAN, PASTOR, AND AFRICAN DIRECTOR OF MAP INTERNATIONAL

Three Specific Problems

At times the problems of Africa seem so overwhelming that hopelessness and despair appear to be the only rational response. But there are powerful reasons not to despair. One is that Jesus Christ is also on the move. As seen earlier, Christianity is growing by leaps and bounds in many African countries. Today there are hundreds of millions of Christians in sub-Saharan Africa. And most of these are evangelicals and Pentecostals who fully accept the basic truths of the Bible. Where the redeeming grace of God is at work, there is reason for hope.

In fact, Christ's church is having a positive impact in many countries and areas of Africa. Take Uganda as one example. In the 1970s it was ruled by a brutal dictator, Idi Amin, who killed an estimated three hundred thousand of his own people and laid waste much of the land. But Christians resisted. Many church leaders spoke out against his regime, even at the cost of their lives. Among these was Anglican Archbishop Janani Luwum who was killed by Idi Amin's henchmen in 1977. Out of the blood of these martyrs, the Ugandan church grew. Today two-thirds of Uganda's population is Christian. The country is largely peaceful and is making strides. Only 12 percent of its urban population lives in poverty. It has reduced the rate of HIV infection from about 20 percent of the population in 1990 to 4.1 percent by 2003.[17] It did so by way of its famous ABC program that stressed sexual **A**bstinence, **B**eing faithful in marriages, and the use of **C**ondoms as a last resort. Churches and other localized, Ugandan agencies were crucial in the success of the ABC program. As in Uganda, African Christians are making a difference in their lands.

In this section I consider three specific, especially crucial problems: HIV/AIDS, malaria, and poverty. How ought we as Christian citizens of the United States react to these problems? What policies ought we to be urging our government to pursue in light of Africa's needs?

"O God, whose Son the Good Shepherd laid down his life for the sheep: We give you thanks for your faithful shepherd, Janani Luwum, who after his Savior's example gave up his life for the people of Uganda. Grant us to be so inspired by his witness that we make no peace with oppression, but live as those who are sealed with the cross of Christ, who died and rose again, and now lives and reigns with you and the Holy Spirit, one God, for ever and ever. Amen."[18]

—EPISCOPAL LECTIONARY PRAYER FOR THE FEAST DAY OF JANANI LUWUM, ARCHBISHOP OF UGANDA AND MARTYR

HIV/AIDS

This dreaded disease has reached catastrophic levels in some, but not all, African countries. As of 2005 the United Nations reports that in Swaziland 33 percent of the people are HIV positive, as are about 20 percent in Botswana, Zimbabwe, Namibia, and South Africa. Only a slightly lower 14 percent are HIV positive in Malawi.[19] There are other countries with infection rates as high or almost as high. As noted earlier, 26 million people are HIV positive in Africa. Many of them will die.

The widespread presence of HIV/AIDS raises three separate issues: stopping the spread of the disease, helping those already infected, and helping orphaned children. What actions ought we as American Christians take in our efforts to live out our solidarity with our fellow human beings in Africa at risk of or already affected by this scourge? What public policies ought we to work for our government to support?

A controversy revolves around the issue of *stopping the spread of HIV/AIDS*. Some believe efforts to stop the spread of HIV/AIDS ought to emphasize sexual abstinence outside of marriage and faithfulness in marriage (the A and B of Uganda's highly effective ABC program). Others believe an equal emphasis—and perhaps even a greater emphasis—should be put on C: the distribution and frank discussion of the use of condoms. Most Christians believe abstinence and faithfulness ought to be the chief thrusts of any efforts to prevent the spread of HIV. Condoms are no absolute guarantee against the spread of the human immunodeficiency virus and, more important, urging their use implicitly sends the message that sexual activities outside of marriage are all right or, at the least, bound to happen. Many believe that emphasizing condom use sends the message that God's standard of sexual purity is an impossibly high standard that most people cannot be expected to live by.

President Bush's program to combat AIDS in Africa (PEPFAR) requires that at least one-third of the money spent to prevent the spread of the virus must be spent on abstinence and faithfulness education. There have been some attempts in Congress to repeal this requirement of the program, but most Christians rightly defend it.

However, Christians who fully understand that this is indeed a broken world where things are often not as they are supposed to be will also recognize that there always have been and there continue to be people who will flout God's standard of sexual chastity. Thus one can argue, on the basis of a Christian understanding of the place of sin in the world, that the C of ABC—that is, the availability and instruction in the use of condoms—must also be a significant part of a program seeking to stop the spread of AIDS.

Also, in male-dominated cultures—as is the case in most African countries—women and girls can be infected with HIV not by sexual promiscuity, but due to the pressures of situations that give them few choices. Husbands who are HIV infected due to their sexual promiscuity often infect their wives. A majority of HIV-infected people in Africa are women, and in some countries married women have higher HIV-infection rates than single women. Girls often enter the sex industry in response to economic and other pressures that seem overwhelming to them. These conditions not only bear witness to the brokenness of our world, but also argue against an abstinence or faithfulness-only approach to stopping the spread of AIDS.

Nevertheless, equally sincere Christians may have differing opinions on how much emphasis to put on abstinence and faithfulness education over and against condom distribution and education. Here we need to be guided by trusted African churches and nongovernmental organizations with direct, local experience. The correct balance may vary from one country or region to another.

The HIV/AIDS crisis in Africa raises a second issue: *how best to care for those who are already infected with HIV or already are suffering from AIDS.* In the United States and other Western countries the lives of people with HIV have been extended—in some cases seemingly indefinitely—by a battery of antiretroviral drugs. Until recently many people had concluded that problems in making these drugs available to most HIV-infected Africans could not be overcome. These drugs were extremely expensive, and they need to be taken in exact dosage levels every day without any interruptions. This requires strong education and distribution systems that were not in place.

But it is becoming clear that antiretroviral drugs can be used in Africa to save thousands, perhaps millions, of lives. The costs of the drugs have come down, as some of them are now available in generic form, and as some drug companies have reduced the price they charge for their drugs going to Africa. Programs treating HIV/AIDS sufferers with antiretroviral drugs in several African countries have demonstrated that the needed educational and distribution networks can be developed. Some 20 percent of Africans in need of antiretroviral drugs are now receiving them[20] But this also means 80 percent are not. People are dying every day who, if they lived in North America or Europe, would not die.

What can we do to help get the needed drugs to those in Africa in desperate need of them? A massive effort is needed. Part of that effort is needed funding. Billions, not millions, of dollars are called for. This is where the American government and those of other Western countries can help. But more than money is needed. Elaborate distribution and education networks are also essential.

Here is where churches and Christian and other nonprofit organizations—both African and American—come into play. They are often the ones that have the trust of the local populace and already have networks extending into even remote villages. Thus they—and we who support them—have a key role to play. This is an especially clear case of the point I made earlier: both civil society and national governments are crucial if needs are to be met and lives saved.

A third issue concerns *the millions of African children being orphaned by AIDS*. There are more than a million AIDS orphans in *each* of these countries: South Africa, Tanzania, Zimbabwe, Kenya, and Uganda.

One response is to redouble efforts to expand antiretroviral drug programs. By extending lives, the number of orphans will be reduced, as HIV-infected parents will be able to continue to care for their own children. But in spite of such efforts, there are already millions of AIDS orphans, and there will be more in the future. Some can be cared for by the extended families of the AIDS victims. But often the extended family has also been ravaged by AIDS. Or it may be so poor that it simply does not have the shelter and food for additional children.

> "The millions upon millions of orphans have now become a heartrending reality. These are individuals whom God personally loves, and we simply cannot abandon them."[21]
>
> —MARK GALLI, MANAGING EDITOR OF *CHRISTIANITY TODAY*

African churches are responding to this crisis through adoptions and orphanages. For example, in Malawi a pastor, T. J. Chipteta, and his wife have started an orphanage called the Home of Hope. With the support of Malawian Christians, it is now serving three hundred orphans. But in a country such as Malawi, which has a per person annual income of only about $160[22] and an estimated 550,000 orphans out of a population of 13 million,[23] it is extremely difficult, if not impossible, for our fellow Christians to meet on their own all the needs of the AIDS orphans. In fact, the Home of Hope orphanage is only surviving with financial support by Christians in the United

States and Canada. It is doing good work, but it is nowhere near adequate to the needs.

Again we face the question of what should be our response as American Christians. The needs are so great that both government assistance programs and the work of individual churches and relief agencies, faith-based and secular, are required. The both-and approach again seems best.

Malaria

Malaria continues to cause hundreds of thousands of deaths each year in Africa. Children under five years of age and expectant mothers are the most vulnerable. As noted earlier, one African child dies from malaria every thirty seconds. Adding to the tragedy is the fact that malaria is preventable. Keys to defeating malaria are insecticide-treated mosquito nets for use while sleeping at night, spraying with insecticides, and treatment with drugs for those who have been infected. None of these poses the problem of prohibitively high costs. A dose of antimalaria drugs costs about one dollar. An insecticide-treated mosquito net costs about ten dollars and can make a huge difference in lives saved. When the United States distributed mosquito nets for every pregnant woman and every child under five years of age in one of the Spice Islands of Zanzibar, the number of malaria cases plunged 90 percent.[24]

In the case of malaria, the problem is not the lack of solutions or of resources with which to implement them. Instead, the problem is one of overcoming indifference and figuring out how to make use of grassroots networks generally already in place. Again, we should look to the relief and development agencies, churches, and other institutions that make up civil society—and to our government with its superior financial resources.

"One million last year alone died on the African continent because of malaria. And in the overwhelming majority of cases, the victims are less than 5 years old, their lives suddenly ended by nothing more than a mosquito bite. The toll of malaria is even more tragic because the disease is highly treatable and preventable . . . the world must take action."[25]

—GEORGE W. BUSH, PRESIDENT OF THE UNITED STATES

Poverty

As seen earlier, poverty is present in overwhelming numbers in Africa. Colonialism, corrupt governments, wars, Western nations' trade policies and their exploitation of Africa's natural resources, disease, a lack of education, and other factors keep many Africans living in deep poverty in spite of their personal hard-working nature and their nations' many natural resources.

We need to be aware of two public-policy issues directly related to poverty in Africa, the first being the trade policies of the United States and other Western nations. It is not so much that we impose high tariffs on goods coming to us from African countries. Instead, it is a matter of the subsidies that our government pays to our farmers. Whenever the American government subsidizes crops such as sugar cane or cotton, it makes it harder for African farmers to compete on the world market with American farm products. The United States spends about $40 billion a year subsidizing American farm products. These subsidies result in lower prices for American farm products—prices that African farmers without the same subsidies have a hard time matching.[26]

There is no neat, obvious, "Christian" answer for the extent to which our government should assist American farmers. Public policy should treat them with justice and enable them to support themselves and their families. But for the Christian citizen, the issue of farm subsidies ought never to be merely a matter of the American farmers' self-interest and the subsidies' impact on our government's budget. We must think how our actions affect African farmers, most of whom are desperately trying to earn a living with which to support themselves and their families. We should also keep in mind that many of them are our fellow believers and that in almost all cases they are much poorer and have fewer options than American farmers.

A second public-policy issue concerns the heavy debt carried by many African governments, resulting from loans granted years ago—often to corrupt dictators—by Western governments, the World Bank, and the International Monetary Fund. Just paying the interest on these loans takes large portions of some countries' budgets, leaving little money for health clinics, schools, and economic development initiatives. For example, in 2005–2006 Kenya spent as much on debt repayments as it spent for water, health, agriculture, roads, transport, and finance combined.[27]

In 2000 the debts of some impoverished countries were cancelled by industrialized countries, but other impoverished countries are still struggling under huge debt burdens.

Many Christians in the United States and in Europe are calling for a "Year of Jubilee," which will result in Western governments and international banking institutions cancelling the debts of poor nations in Africa and elsewhere. These Christians point to Leviticus 25 and the year of jubilee the Israelites were instructed to observe, when all the land that had been sold would be returned to their original owners and all debts cancelled. There is a biblical basis for forgiving loans. But others have argued that simply forgiving the debts of nations will encourage irresponsible rulers to enter into new debts, hoping they too will never need to be paid. Forgiving debts, they point out, is a bad precedent that rewards irresponsible behavior.

> "The world's most impoverished countries are forced to pay over $100 million EVERY DAY to the rich world in debt repayments, while poverty kills millions of their people."[28]
>
> —JUBILEE DEBT CAMPAIGN

It seems to me that the right thing to do is to forgive a nation's debts that were entered into by irresponsible rulers years ago, often with the overly quick and easy approval of the lending nation, and that are now imposing a crushing burden on the debtor countries. But others will disagree. No matter what position we take, it should be motivated by a genuine, heartfelt concern for the peoples of these countries. We ought not merely insist—as did the ungrateful servant in Christ's parable in Matthew 18:23–35—that what is legally owed must be paid irrespective of the dire circumstances of the debtor.

Conclusion

A final word: The biggest danger in regard to Africa and its needs is not that Americans as a whole, the news media, or members of Congress will come out forcefully against aiding orphans, fighting against malaria, or stopping the spread of AIDS. The real danger is that the American population's and Congress's attention will drift elsewhere, and programs of assistance will languish. We who hold the lives of all people as being precious in God's sight—no matter what their race, no matter where they live—need to continue to press for action by our churches and our overseas relief and development agencies. And by our government. This is not a one- or two-year battle against disease and poverty; a major, long-term, year-in and year-out effort is needed. Africa must not be the "fad" for a year or two. Consistent, sustained acts of love and concern are needed, undertaken by individual Christians and their churches, Christian relief and development agencies, and—encouraged and spurred on by Christian citizens—our government's policies toward Africa.

Question for Reflection and Discussion

1. Christianity is probably growing faster in Africa than anywhere else in the world. Do you think this increases our responsibility as American Christians to try to do more to respond to the tragic problems Africa is facing? Why or why not?

2. As Americans become aware of the problems Africa is facing, they can react with despair: We'll never be able to make a difference. Do you tend to react this way? Try to think of some ways you could perhaps make a difference. Think in terms of what you can do both as an individual Christian and as a citizen of the United States.

3. Do you think programs aimed to stop the spread of HIV should focus only on abstinence and faithfulness education, or should condom distribution and education also be a part of our efforts? How does your Christian faith affect your position on this issue?

4. Do you think American trade policies should encourage the development of African agriculture and industry, even if they cost Americans some jobs? How does your Christian faith affect your answer?

12

War and Terrorism

"The Lord Is My Strength and My Defense"

(Exodus 15:2, TNIV)

ALONG WITH ALMOST ALL AMERICANS, I vividly remember where I was and what I was doing the morning of September 11, 2001. I lived in California at the time. I had my radio alarm set for 6 A.M.—9 A.M. in the east—and the news came on as I was waking up. There were vague reports of an airplane crashing into one of the World Trade Center towers in New York City. I assumed that in foul weather a small private plane had accidentally crashed into one of the towers and did not think too much of it. I went about my daily routine.

But before I was out of the shower, my wife informed me that a second plane had crashed into the second World Trade Center tower. I immediately sensed these were terrorist attacks and that something dreadful was going on. My wife and I watched with mounting horror as we saw television images of the two towers burning, and then one after the other crashing to the ground. Horror was added to horror as we heard of another plane crashing into the Pentagon and of a fourth crashing into a Pennsylvania field.

I suspect all of us were as moved as we were that day because, even though we are not strangers to violence, this was something new. We

194

read daily of automobile crashes that take lives; we can put natural disasters such as tornadoes that take lives into an understandable category; we even have, after a fashion, come to accept the random violence of street crime. But this was different. This was a planned, coordinated attack on the United States.

Since 9/11 of 2001, there have been other attacks linked to terrorists affiliated with the same radical Islam as the 9/11 attackers: In 2002, 180 were killed in the bombing of a Bali night club in Indonesia; in 2004, 191 were killed in a Madrid train bombing; in 2005, 52 were killed in London transit attacks. In 2006 a plot to blow up as many as ten airplanes over the Atlantic was uncovered just in time.

How are we as Christians to react to cruel terrorist attacks against civilian targets designed to take as many lives as possible? We are told to forgive our enemies and to turn the other cheek. But did our Lord mean to include twenty-first-century terrorists? God has established governments to pursue justice in this world and to punish wrongdoers. Surely terrorists who indiscriminately take human lives must be included in the wrongdoers whom governments are called to punish. But exactly what does this mean in terms of the antiterrorist policies our government should pursue?

These are the questions I consider in this chapter. I first discuss how the key biblical principles we have been considering throughout this book relate to the question of war and terrorism. In the next section I suggest how to apply these principles to the ongoing struggle our country is waging in an effort to stop the evil intentions of terrorists and keep us all safe.

Key Biblical Principles

Creation, Sin, Redemption

In 1989 the world heaved a sigh of relief and looked forward to better days. The unbelievable had happened. The Berlin Wall fell. Then, first in East Germany, followed by one country of Eastern Europe after another, communist governments fell and jubilant crowds jammed city squares as freedom replaced repression. Next the Soviet Union itself crumbled; its non-Russian provinces gained their independence, and free market and democratic reforms swept through

Russia. The long Cold War struggle against the Soviet Union and its communist ideology had ended with victory for the West and the forces of freedom.

We all rejoiced, thanked God, and looked forward to an era of peace and security. But it was not to be. Soon war and ethnic cleansing broke out in the Balkans. American armed forces were fighting in the deserts of the Middle East to repel Saddam Hussein's invasion of Kuwait. Rwanda experienced genocide as Hutu extremist groups slaughtered some eight hundred thousand Tutsis and moderate Hutus. And then came 9/11, other terrorist attacks, and wars in Afghanistan and Iraq. North Korea and Iran are moving to acquire nuclear weapons. Russia is slipping back into authoritarianism. Today some even look back nostalgically to the more stable patterns of the Cold War years.

But we ought not to be surprised. Christ himself warned that there would be "wars and rumors of wars" until his coming again in power (Matt. 24:6). The reality of sin in the world and the pride and selfishness that tend to mark nations—and our own hearts—all too easily degenerate into a love of power and an overwhelming pride in one's own nation or one's own ethnic or religious group.

Without a clear understanding of human sinfulness that reaches into all of our hearts, it is easy to imagine that if only we get rid of a communist Soviet Union or an especially evil ruler, such as Saddam Hussein or a terrorist mastermind such as Osama bin Laden, peace will reign on earth. We will all live in security. But such thinking denies the Christian teaching of sin. Evil is not centered in one especially evil regime or one especially evil ruler. As we saw in chapter 2, it is everywhere, because it is lodged in each human heart, and thus is present in every nation.

This sounds like a council of despair. However, the story does not end with sin and evil. God has not abandoned the world, but is still active in it. In Jesus Christ God has sent a Savior to redeem the world and to right what has gone so very wrong. The results are all around us. There are world leaders and regimes that are peaceful, seek the welfare of their neighbors, and work to stop the evils others are perpetrating. When a natural disaster strikes, such as the tsunami that flooded parts of south Asia in December 2004, other nations, our own included, rush in with assistance. Good and evil are both present in our world, and there is a constant, ongoing struggle between them. Through it all, God is in control.

In the times between Christ's coming to redeem the world and his second coming in power to make all things right, we are called to work as God's peacemakers. We are to avoid a naïve optimism that thinks shalom will come by the efforts of our or any other country; we are also to avoid a deep pessimism that thinks all our efforts to stem violence and bring peace will be futile.

Solidarity

Immediately following 9/11 the Paris newspaper *Le Monde* carried this headline: "We Are All Americans Now." In the United States the slogan "united we stand" suddenly appeared on billboards, bumper stickers, and other public places. Both the French headline and the slogan illustrate the principle of solidarity. In the face of brutal terrorist attacks, the French newspaper was saying we are one with you Americans in your grief and loss. "United we stand" proclaimed that all Americans stood with New York, Washington, and all who had suffered loss. An attack on some was taken to be an attack on all.

Solidarity means standing together in a unity of concern and help with those who have suffered harm. Even today many risk their own lives to root out terrorist cells and capture those involved in terrorist activities. They devise new means to spot terrorist attacks before they occur and in other ways oppose wanton killing by al Qaeda and other modern-day terrorists. They are acting in solidarity with those they are seeking to protect.

Surely we as Christians need to identify with the victims of terrorist attacks—whether our own citizens killed on 9/11 or those in

> "We are all Americans! We are all New Yorkers, just as surely as John F. Kennedy declared himself to be a Berliner in 1962 when he visited Berlin. Indeed, just as in the gravest moments of our own history, how can we not feel profound solidarity with those people, that country, the United States, to whom we are so close and to whom we owe our freedom, and therefore our solidarity?"[1]
>
> —JEAN-MARIE COLOMBANI, *LE MONDE*, SEPTEMBER 12, 2001

other parts of the world. Indifference—an attitude of "I'm glad I'm not affected"—is not an option for us.

Justice

It surely is just to protect men, women, and children from death such as almost three thousand of our fellow citizens suffered on 9/11. This is a part of government's God-given duty to promote a just order in society. But how does a government root out potential terrorists before they act and punish those who have engaged in terrorist acts—*in a just manner?* Here is where we need to do some careful thinking. As we urge our government both to seek justice by rooting out terrorist threats and to do so in a just manner, it is important for us to keep in mind four perspectives rooted in God's Word. The first is that *our country and its government are themselves far from perfect and prone to make errors and to act from improper motives.* When in 2002 President George W. Bush referred to an "axis of evil" that included Saddam Hussein's Iraq, Iran, and North Korea, he was criticized for making sweeping, moralistic judgments. But if Saddam's government in Iraq was not an evil regime, and if the governments of Iran and North Korea are not evil regimes today, I do not know what evil is. Thousands have died under these brutal, repressive regimes, and they have threatened their neighbors with death and destruction.

But an additional biblically rooted perspective needs to be recognized as well. Chapter 2 quoted Solzhenitsyn as saying, "the line dividing good and evil cuts through the heart of every human being." This is a profound truth rooted in Scripture: "All have sinned and fall short of the glory of God" (Rom. 3:23). We evangelicals readily acknowledge this truth, but we often miss its full implications.

If this is true of every human heart, it is also true of every government—including our own. That is why from our founding we have relied on a system of divided powers and checks and balances to keep our government restrained. We rightly fear unlimited governmental power, because we understand that government can become a force for evil as well as a force for good. But we Americans seem to recognize this truth and its implications more quickly in the case of domestic policies than in the case of foreign policies, and especially policies dealing with war and peace. Then we often too quickly give the benefit of the doubt to our leaders.

Fighting al Qaeda and other terrorists who would attack us requires an active, powerful government; the potential for wrong doing that lies in all of our hearts requires restraints be put on that same government.

A second important perspective grows out of the first: *Basic human rights must be protected even as we struggle against terrorists* who would destroy us. The United States has worked to protect human rights by writing them into the civil liberties protected by the Bill of Rights and other legal codes. If in fighting terrorists we do away with protections for our basic civil liberties, the terrorists will have already won. We face a ruthless enemy and some additional powers for our authorities are needed, if they are to be successful in protecting us. But the evil that lies within the hearts of all—including our own authorities—requires curbs on those new powers.

> "If angels were to govern, neither external nor internal controls on government would be necessary. In framing a government which is to be administered by men over men, the great difficulty lies in this: you must first enable the government to control the governed; and in the next place oblige it to control itself."[2]
>
> —JAMES MADISON, FOUNDING FATHER AND FOURTH PRESIDENT

In addition, the torture of terrorists to extract information and the holding of *suspected* terrorists in prisons for years is unjust. Both of which, sadly, have been acts in which our government has engaged since 9/11. Terrorists and those suspected of having ties to terrorists are also God's image bearers with God-given human rights that no one—including our authorities—should violate.

In the struggle against terrorism it is easy for a pragmatic mind-set to take over. If by some "mild" forms of torture, we may be able to extract information that will save hundreds, even thousands, of lives, is this not something we should do? If someone may be a key in the al Qaeda network, should we not hold him indefinitely, even if we may later prove to be wrong? After all, thousands of American lives could be at stake. But such thinking is wrong.

In our personal lives, we recognize a pragmatic, the-end-justifies-the-means mind-set is wrong. I recall, early in my teaching career, catching a student plagiarizing material and handing it in as his own.

When I confronted him with what he had done, he admitted it, but he further explained that he had become so busy teaching Sunday school and attending other church activities, that he had run out of time to do his own work! Teaching Sunday school is commendable, as is earning good grades on one's school work. But God is concerned not only with what we achieve, but with how we go about achieving it. Both must be in keeping with his will.

It is similar for nations. Using the end to justify any means is as wrong for nations as it is in our personal lives. Our country ought to pursue justice by protecting us from terrorists who would kill indiscriminately. But in doing so we must not act unjustly toward those who oppose us.

A third perspective, deeply rooted in the Bible and Christian history, is *the just-war theory*. It originated in the thinking of Augustine more than 1,500 years ago and has been accepted, with some variations, by most Christians ever since. It sets down six conditions if military action is to meet the biblical standard of justice. They are as follows:

"Torture violates the basic dignity of the human person that all religions, in their highest ideals, hold dear. It degrades everyone involved—policy-makers, perpetrators and victims. It contradicts our nation's most cherished values. Any policies that permit torture and inhumane treatment are shocking and morally intolerable. . . . Let America abolish torture now—without exceptions."[3]

—A 2006 STATEMENT SIGNED BY MANY EVANGELICAL AND OTHER RELIGIOUS LEADERS

1. Just cause. Military force may be used only to defend against an external attack or to respond to a grave evil and those who are committing it.

2. Comparative justice. Recognizing that there are usually injustices on both sides in a dispute, the injustice being suffered by one party must clearly outweigh the injustice being suffered by the other.

3. Legitimate authority. Only properly constituted governments, not individuals or nongovernmental groups, may use military action.

4. Right intention. Military force may be used only to correct the grave injustice that has been committed—not for material gain or other advantages.

5. Probability of success. Military force may not be used in support of a futile cause or where the destruction that is likely outweighs the good to be achieved.

6. Last resort. Military force may be used only when all other means of achieving success have been tried and have failed.

Just-war theory rests on two foundations. One is that governments are instituted by God for a special role in human society. Governments are to promote justice and punish wrongdoers, and in so doing are allowed to "bear the sword" (Rom. 13:4). There are things governments may do in pursuit of justice that no individual may do. This we saw earlier in chapter 3. The second foundation is that governments may not rush off to war quickly or easily. In God's sight, war is something to be avoided if at all possible. It is an awesome act that reveals as nothing else the brokenness of our world.

Just-war theory is the beginning not the end of our thinking about how our nation can, in a Christian manner, respond to the challenge terrorism presents. It forms a basis for the American government to engage in war and warlike actions; it also raises many cautions or warning flags.

A fourth and final Christian perspective important for a just struggle against terrorists is *forgiveness*. In October 2006 the world was shocked when a man entered an Amish school in Pennsylvania, separated the boys from the girls, tied the girls up, and began to execute them one by one. He killed five girls before killing himself. But the world was even more shocked when the Amish community that had been subjected to unimaginable violence met with the widow of the man who had killed their children, forgave her for what had happened, and even expressed solidarity with her by attending the funeral of her husband, who had caused them untold sorrow. How could those who had been deeply violated act on the basis not of vengeance or cold indifference, but of love and forgiveness?

We Christians know the answer—even when we as individuals struggle to live up to the will of our Savior. Christ has taught us to pray, "Forgive us our debts, as we forgive our debtors" (Matt. 6:12, KJV). Forgiveness—even of our enemies—is the hard but undeniable burden our Lord has put on us. This also is a matter of justice. One thing that is due the terrorists who have sworn to destroy us is forgiveness.

The Application of Biblical Principles

The War on Terror

On September 14, 2001, three days after the al Qaeda attacks on the United States, President George W. Bush mounted the steps to the pulpit at the National Cathedral in Washington, D.C., and delivered one of the most heartfelt and moving addresses of his presidency: "We are here in the middle hour of our grief. So many have suffered so great a loss, and today we express our nation's sorrow. We come before God to pray for the missing and the dead, and for those who love them."

But later in the same address he made this statement: "But our responsibility to history is already clear: to answer these attacks and rid the world of evil."[4] Six days later, before a joint session of Congress, he said, "Our war on terror begins with al Qaeda, but it does not end there. It will not end until every terrorist group of global reach has been found, stopped and defeated."[5] It is necessary to ponder these words carefully—and in light of the principles of a broken world, solidarity, and justice.

War was clearly forced upon us on September 11, 2001. In fact, Osama bin Laden had issued a statement years earlier that was in effect a declaration of war. Al Qaeda represents an evil that it is right for our government to oppose with all our might; solidarity requires all of us to rally to the defense of those who are threatened; and, after having been attacked, there is a just cause as demanded by just-war theory.

Yet questions can be raised concerning the latter two statements of President Bush. They seem to promise a war that is nearly open-ended in its reach and goals. Is it really possible to "rid the world of evil" in a broken, sinful world? The Bible teaches this will come about only when Christ returns in power and every knee will bow before him (Phil. 2:10; Rom. 14:11). Even if we do not take the president's words literally, do they not reveal a mind-set that can easily slip into thinking that by our efforts we can bring about a world without the sort of evils that will always be present in a sinful world?

The quotation from President Bush's address to a joint session of Congress promised a war on terror that reaches beyond the al Qaeda organization that attacked us to include "every terrorist group of global reach." This raises a crucial question we need to weigh carefully: Is the "war on terror" a true war, similar to World War II, or is it a war in the sense of an intense struggle, strenuous efforts, and sacrifices? We sometimes think of wars in the second sense. Our leaders have at times announced "a war on drugs," "a war on crime," or even "a war on poverty." Is this the sort of war we are in? Or is this a real war, with identified enemies, battlefields, and military forces?

These are not merely theoretical questions professors might pose to a freshman class to get students thinking. Their practical consequences are enormous. Either type of war potentially can be justified under biblical principles. But these same principles also teach that governments can be perverted to wrong ends. That is why James Madison insisted on a system of checks and balances. If this is true, there is no occasion when a sense of caution and checks and balances are more needed than when a government exercises the power to make war militarily or to exercise its police power to catch, prosecute, and perhaps execute evildoers.

But what sort of war is the war on terror? If it is a war in a literal sense, it would be limited by having a clearly defined enemy and by the rules of war. Presumably the enemy is al Qaeda. After all, it is the organization that attacked us on 9/11. Should President Bush have asked Congress for a formal declaration of war against al Qaeda? And, if he concluded the threat went beyond al Qaeda, against other, named terrorist organizations or states? If this had been done, it would have limited and focused the actions of our nation and military. There would have been a clearly defined enemy. In addition, the rules of war, such as the Geneva Convention, would clearly have been an obligation on us and might have prevented the unjust use of torture. It would have given our military the clear legal authority to hold members and sympathizers of al Qaeda as prisoners of war until a peace settlement had been reached.

Or is the war on terror not a literal war, but a war-like struggle against evil forces, similar to an ongoing "war" against drug dealers or organized crime? If this is the case, the power of our government would again be limited. This time it would be limited by the rights promised under the Bill of Rights to all Americans and aliens living in our country who are suspected or accused of crimes.

There are dangers in waging a war on terror without either (1) clearly declaring war on a specified country or organization, or (2) making clear that this "war" is against an international band of criminal thugs who are to be brought to justice by means of a vigorous use of the tools available to the criminal-justice system. The dangers arise from the government picking and choosing what rules apply to it and what tactics to use—at times acting as though this is a literal war and at times as though it is a hunt for especially vicious international criminals. Our war on terror is more likely to be fought in a just manner, if we would clearly answer this question one way or the other.

What kind of a war is this then? What kind of war ought it to be? On these questions Christians can and will differ. A case can be made either way. The important thing is that we conscientiously seek to answer such questions based on biblical principles and perspectives, not simply on national pride, fear, or a pragmatic acceptance of whatever we believe will stop terrorism.

Afghanistan and Iraq

There can be no doubt that by almost any definition the United States is involved in a real war in Afghanistan and Iraq. Fighting is ongoing and soldiers are dying. No doubt some who are reading these words have lost in these wars family members whom they loved more than life itself. For them—and for all of us who stand in solidarity with them—the continuing wars in Afghanistan and Iraq are real, tragic, and bitter. But also perhaps necessary and just. That is what I consider in this section. How ought we as Christian believers evaluate our country's actions in these far-off countries?

We need to consider two sets of questions in terms of both of these countries. First, were our original invasions of these countries justified on biblical principles? Both countries had what clearly were evil regimes. The Taliban in Afghanistan oppressed women, persecuted Christians, and in other ways violated human rights—and actively gave aid and sanctuary to those who attacked the United States on 9/11. The Saddam Hussein regime in Iraq earlier attacked its neighbor Kuwait and cruelly oppressed many of its own people, especially the Kurds in the north and the majority Shiite Muslims in the south. The world had reason to believe that it possessed weapons of mass destruction.

It is easier to justify the attack on the Taliban regime in Afghanistan than the attack on Iraq, because the Taliban were clearly harboring and giving assistance to the very organization that attacked us. In addition, the United States had broad international support for its attack on Afghanistan. Were these enough to judge that our attack had a just cause, right intentions, a high probability of success, and legitimate authority? Did it meet the other terms of just-war theory? I personally answer these questions with a yes, but others may disagree.

But what about Iraq? Here the ties to the 9/11 attacks were tenuous, even though the evils of the Saddam regime were clear enough. The potential for Iraq to be involved in future terrorist attacks was present and serious, especially given the general belief that it had weapons of mass destruction. Was this enough to create a "just cause"? Was the presence of oil—something not present in Afghanistan—perhaps a factor that helped lead us to war, thereby violating the "right intent" point of just-war theory? Equally sincere Christians can disagree on the conclusions they reach to such questions.

But our political and military leaders made a basic error in Iraq that a fuller understanding of Christian principles would have helped prevent. Our postwar policy seemingly was governed by a naïve optimism concerning human nature that has more to do with modern secularist assumptions than with biblical teachings. In Iraq especially, we went in and removed the existing regime, disbanded the armed forces, and did away with most of the civil authorities—and apparently expected that a peaceful, lawful society would spring up in their stead. The error was to assume—probably unself-consciously—that all evil was concentrated in the Saddam regime. Get rid of it, and peace and cooperation would flourish.

But we Christians know better—or at least should know better. Remove an existing government and criminal elements and a selfish pride in one's own religious and ethnic group are more likely to flourish than peace and cooperation. Thousands of American troops and uncounted thousands of Iraqis have paid with their lives for the naïveté of our leaders. To go into Iraq and remove an existing regime—as evil as what it was—without effective plans to replace it with a more just order, violated just war's fifth point, that of probable success. It says that for a war to be just, the good likely to be achieved by it must outweigh the destruction that is likely to be caused by the war.

The second question asks: what to do now? We removed Saddam with no workable plan for what was to come after, resulting in lawlessness and sectarian violence. One can argue that to pull out now, leaving a worse, bloodier situation than when we came is both wrong and against the long-term chances for a more peaceful world. But one can also argue there is not much we can do. Religious and ethnic jealousies can only be moderated by the Iraqis themselves. If peace and stability are to come, the various Iraqi factions must put aside revenge, forgiving past wrongs, and commit to working together. Economics also enter in. Iraq's oil lies in the Kurdish north and the Shiite south, and none lies in the predominantly Sunni areas. If leaders of the Kurds and Shiites would step forward and agree to share their oil wealth with the Sunni areas, the ground could be laid for an end to the violence.

If, however, there are no Iraqi leaders willing to forgive past wrongs and to share equitably Iraq's oil resources, there may not be much we can do to stop the violence. Withdrawal and an admission of past errors may then be the best option. We as a nation would be humbled, and many Iraqis would suffer due to our errors. But when we, either as individuals or as a nation, have made a grievous mistake that cannot be repaired, the best answer may be to admit the mistake, ask for forgiveness, and work to learn from one's error.

Others will conclude that the situation in Iraq can yet be salvaged. And they will feel we owe it to the Iraqis to continue trying to do so. There indeed are many Iraqis who desire to create a democratic, peaceful government that unites all Iraqis. Are we now simply to abandon them? We need to stand in solidarity with the suffering Iraqis and help them overcome those who seek power by way of murder and mayhem.

When we as Christian citizens debate such issues, we need to be guided by a realistic understanding of sin in a broken world that is not as it is supposed to be, by a loving concern for our neighbors in Iraq, and by a full commitment to justice. We should be guided by biblical perspectives such as these, not by national self-interest and pride, political advantage, and access to natural resources.

The Patriot Act

On October 26, 2001—only forty-six days after 9/11—Congress passed and President Bush signed into law the USA Patriot Act. In 2006 Congress renewed the legislation, after amending some of its provisions. It has aroused much controversy. Some claim it is essential for catching terrorists and potential terrorists in our midst. They add that it does no more than grant the same powers to law enforcement authorities in their efforts to catch terrorists as they have always had in catching drug dealers and organized-crime figures. Others claim it dangerously concentrates power in the hands of law enforcement officials who could easily misuse their new powers. The privacy of every American, they argue, is being put at risk.

A reading of the actual USA Patriot Act or even of the many arguments made for and against it is guaranteed to give a headache to all but the most dedicated lawyers! What are concerned Christian citizens to do? They want their families and their fellow Americans to be safe from terrorist attacks. But they also realize the danger posed by unbridled governmental power. How can we understand even the broad scope of the Patriot Act and sort out claims from the counterclaims and reach a conscientious position?

A basic principle needs to be applied here: When power is concentrated in one person or one agency, with no independent limit or check on that power, it is very likely, sooner or later, to be abused. As I have emphasized at various points, God has established governments as his agents for a more just order in society. But in a broken, sinful world governments themselves are prone to become agents of injustice. That is why it is important to limit governmental powers; when power is given to a governmental agency, provision ought to be made for others to know what it is doing and to be able to block or curb its use of that power.

The key question we should ask of the Patriot Act—as well as of other antiterrorist powers various government agencies have been given—is not simply whether new, sweeping powers have been given to certain intelligence-gathering and law-enforcement agencies; we should ask whether those new powers are accompanied by independent checks on those agencies. Are there other agencies that are looking over the shoulders of those exercising the new powers?

For the most part, the answer seems to be yes in the case of the Patriot Act. There is, for example, a federal court called the Foreign Intelligence Surveillance Court (FISC), created specifically to oversee the work of agencies involved in foreign intelligence work. It must approve most wiretaps or other surveillance work of these agencies. And this court is independent, composed of eleven federal district court judges who are appointed by the chief justice of the Supreme Court for seven-year terms. In recent years it has in fact turned down numerous requests for surveillance activities.

But others have concluded that the checks on the powers of antiterrorism offices are insufficient. They expressed special concern over the Protect America Act of 2007 that limited certain oversight powers of the FISC. They have also argued there are certain types of surveillance activities no governmental agency should engage in, even if there are independent checks.

I have neither the need nor the wisdom to judge here who is correct in this ongoing debate. From a Christian perspective, I insist that the key need is for effective, independent checks on the authority of the law enforcement and surveillance agencies. That is the question we need to ask and for which we need to obtain answers. That is the best means to ensure against both the injustice of terrorists spreading death and destruction and the injustice of innocent civilians being subjected to police-state intrusions into their privacy.

Conclusion

If we Christians follow basic biblical principles relevant to the world of governments and public policies to the best our abilities, our way of thinking about, reacting to, and evaluating public policies will be radically altered. We will no longer be conformed to the pattern of this world and its way of thinking, but will be transformed by the renewing of our minds (Rom. 12:2). This does not mean that all of us will always agree on all issues. Far from it. Nowhere is that more true than in the case of the awesome issues of war and terrorism considered in this chapter. But this is not a reason for despair. God is sovereign; he is in control. He will use our transformed minds to accomplish his purposes. And no one can hope for anything better than this.

Questions for Reflection and Discussion

1. Do you have more faith and confidence in our government when it comes to fighting terrorism than you do when it comes to domestic issues such as welfare or environmental policies? Why or why not? If you answered yes, do you think this is an inconsistency you should work to change, or is there a good reason for your different levels of confidence?

2. Do you think the six points that make up the just-war theory are biblically based and helpful in today's world?

3. Forgiveness is surely a Christian virtue. How might this change the world situation, if it were more faithfully followed by us as Christian citizens, by our nation, and by other nations?

4. Do you think the war on terror is a literal war, as was World War II, or is it a serious, warlike struggle against the evil of terrorist attacks? What should it be? Why does the chapter claim it is important for our nation to answer to this question clearly?

Notes

Chapter 1: Our Starting Point

1. Three of the better biographies on Wilberforce and on which most of this example is based are Kevin Belmonte, *Hero for Humanity: A Biography of William Wilberforce* (Colorado Springs, CO: NavPress, 2002); Garth Lean, *God's Politician* (Colorado Springs, CO: Helmers & Howard, 1987); and Eric Metaxas, *Amazing Grace: William Wilberforce and the Heroic Campaign to End Slavery* (San Francisco: HarperSanFrancisco, 2007).

2. John Newton, quoted in British Broadcasting Corporation, Religion and Ethics—Christianity, "William Wilberforce," www.bbc.co.uk/religion/religions/christianity/people/williamwilberforce_2.shtml.

3. Frederick Douglass, quoted in Belmonte, *Hero for Humanity*, p. 19.

4. Richard Land, quoted in Michael Foust, " 'Amazing Grace' Film about Wilberforce Called Inspirational," *Baptist Press*, www.bpnews.net/bpnews.asp?ID=24883.

5. For more information, see Vishal and Ruth Mangalwadi, *The Legacy of William Carey* (Wheaton, IL: Crossway Books, 1999), esp. pp. 82–88.

6. See William Martin, *With God on Our Side: The Rise of the Religious Right in America* (New York: Broadway Books, 1996), pp. 69–70.

7. Ed Dobson, in Cal Thomas and Ed Dobson, *Blinded by Might: Why the Religious Right Can't Save America* (Grand Rapids, MI: Zondervan, 1999), p. 50.

8. William Wilberforce, *Real Christianity Contrasted with the Prevailing Religious System*, abridged and edited by James M. Houston (Portland, OR: Multnomah, 1982).

9. Cal Thomas, in Thomas and Dobson, *Blinded by Might*, pp. 143–44, quoting *New York Times*, February 12, 1998.

10. David Kuo, *Tempting Faith: The Inside Story of Political Seduction* (New York: The Free Press, 2006), p. 173.

Chapter 2: Creation, Sin, and Redemption

1. Cornelius Plantinga Jr., *Not the Way It's Supposed to Be: A Breviary of Sin* (Grand Rapids, MI: Eerdmans, 1995).

2. Albert M. Wolters, *Creation Regained: Biblical Basis for a Reformational Worldview* (Grand Rapids, MI: Eerdmans, 1985), p. 39.

3. For more on shalom, see Nicholas Wolterstorff, *Until Justice and Peace Embrace* (Grand Rapids, MI: Eerdmans, 1983), pp. 69–72.

4. Aleksandr Solzhenitsyn, quoted in Cornelius Plantinga Jr., *Engaging God's World* (Grand Rapids, MI: Eerdmans, 2002), p. 49.

5. Plantinga, *Not the Way It's Supposed to Be*, p. 199.
6. Cornelius Plantinga Jr., *Engaging God's World*, p. 98.
7. Abraham Kuyper, "Sphere Sovereignty," quoted in James D. Bratt, ed., *Abraham Kuyper: A Centennial Reader* (Grand Rapids, MI: Eerdmans, 1998), p. 488.
8. Wolters, *Creation Regained*, p. 58.

Chapter 3: Justice

1. Bono (address, National Prayer Breakfast, Washington, DC, February 2, 2006), American Rhetoric Online Speech Bank, www.americanrhetoric.com/speeches/bononationalprayer-breakfast.htm.
2. Charles Colson, with Anne Morse, "What Is Justice?" *Christianity Today*, August 2005, p. 80.
3. Governor Bob Riley, quoted in Brainy Quote, "Bob Riley Quotes," www.brainyquote.com/quotes/authors/b/bob_riley.html.
4. Susan Pace Hamill, *The Least of These: Fair Taxes and the Moral Duty of Christians* (Birmingham: Sweet Water Press, 2003), p. ix.
5. Cal Thomas, in Cal Thomas and Ed Dobson, *Blinded by Might: Why the Religious Right Can't Save America* (Grand Rapids, MI: Zondervan, 1999), p. 95.

Chapter 4: Solidarity

1. Diet Eman, with James C. Schaap, *Things We Couldn't Say* (Grand Rapids, MI: Eerdmans, 1994), p. 373. "Making Choices: The Dutch Resistance During World War II," a DVD on Christians involved in the Dutch Resistance in World War II, which contains extensive interviews with Diet Eman, is also available from Robert Prince at Rob.Prince@uaf.edu.
2. Eman, *Things We Couldn't Say*, p. 90.
3. Pope John Paul II, *Sollicitude Rei Socialis* [On Social Concerns] (1987), sec. 40.
4. For more information on Habitat for Humanity and the boxed quotation, see www.habitat.org/how/factsheet.aspx.
5. Arthur Brooks, *Who Really Cares?* (New York: Basic Books, 2006).
6. "Free Abdul Rahman," an editorial in the *Washington Times*, March 23, 2006.

Chapter 5: Civil Society

1. For an account of the Riveras' conflict over home schooling their daughter and other similar cases, see Home School Legal Defense Association, www.hslda.org/hs/state/tx/200602010.asp.
2. For more background on civil society, see Don E. Eberly, ed., *The Essential Civil Society Reader* (Lanham, MD: Rowman and Littlefield, 2000).
3. Kim Lawton, "Katrina Faith-Based Funding Controversy," *Religion and Ethics Newsweekly*, February 10, 2006, www.pbs.org/wnet/religionandethics/week924/cover.html.
4. For more on Abraham Kuyper's conversion and life, see Frank Vanden Berg, *Abraham Kuyper* (Grand Rapids, MI: Eerdmans, 1960); and Kuyper's own account of his conversion: "Confidentiality," in James D. Bratt, ed., *Abraham Kuyper: A Centennial Reader* (Grand Rapids, MI: Eerdmans, 1998), pp. 45–61.
5. Kuyper, "Confidentiality," p. 54.
6. For more background on sphere sovereignty, subsidiarity, and similar concepts, see David T. Koyzis, *Political Visions and Illusions* (Downers Grove, IL: InterVarsity Press, 2003), ch. 8; Stephen V. Monsma, *Positive Neutrality* (Westport, CT: Greenwood, 1996), ch. 4; and, from a Catholic perspective, J. Bryan Hehir, "Religious Ideas and Social Policy: Subsidiarity and Catholic Style of Ministry," in Mary Jo Bane, Brent Coffin, and Ronald Thiemann, eds., *Who Will Provide? The Changing Role of Religion in American Social Welfare* (Boulder, CO: Westview, 2000), pp. 97–120.

7. "The Responsive Communitarian Platform," *The Responsive Community* 2 (Winter 1991–1992): 4. *The Responsive Community* is published by the Institute for Communitarian Studies, a secular organization, but one that gives an appropriate emphasis on the importance of social institutions and communities.

8. Alan Feuer and Thomas J. Lueck, "Long Chain of Alarms Preceded Death of Girl, 7," *New York Times*, January 13, 2006.

9. Justice James C. McReynolds, from his majority opinion in *Pierce v. Society of the Sisters of the Holy Names of Jesus and Mary*, 268 U.S. 510 at 534–535 (1925).

10. Freedom from Religion Foundation, www.ffrf.org/(accessed November, 11, 2006).

11. Witches Voice, www.witchvox.com/.

Chapter 6: Church and State

1. See "Alabama Ousts Justice Moore," *WorldNetDaily*, November 13, 2003, www.world-netdaily.com/news/article.asp?ARTICLE_ID=35566. The Judge Moore quotation can be found at www.cnn.com/2003/LAW/11/13/moore.tencommandments.

2. *Rosenberger v. Rector*, 515 U.S. 819 at 839 (1995).

3. Justice Potter Stewart, from his dissenting opinion in *Abington School District v. Schempp*, 374 U.S. 203, at 319–320 (1963).

4. Justice Clarence Thomas, from his majority opinion in *Good News Club v. Milford Central School*, 533 U.S. 98 at 99 (2001).

5. A. James Reichley, *Religion in American Public Life* (Washington, DC: Brookings, 1990), p. 165.

6. *Van Orden v. Perry*, 545 U.S. 677 (2005).

7. *McCreary County v. ACLU of Kentucky*, 545 U.S. 849 (2005).

8. Justice Sandra Day O'Connor, from her opinion in *Westside Community Schools v. Mergens*, 496 U.S. 226, at 252 (1990).

9. Chief Justice William H. Rehnquist, from the majority opinion in *Zelman v. Simmons-Harris*, 536 U.S. 639, at 662–663 (2002).

Chapter 7: Life Issues

1. For more information on the 2005 Terri Schiavo case, the online Wikipedia Encyclopedia has a balanced, accurate account, under "Terri Schiavo," http://en.wikipedia.org/wiki/Terri_Schiavo (accessed June 7, 2006).

2. Basic information on fetal development can be found in medical books and on many Web sites. Especially helpful: Christopher Vaughan, *How Life Begins: The Science of Life in the Womb* (New York: Random House, 1996).

3. Vaughan, *How Life Begins*, pp. 77–78.

4. Westside Pregnancy Resource Center, www.wprc.org/testimonials.phtml (accessed February 19, 2007).

5. Don Piper with Cecil Murphey, *90 Minutes in Heaven* (Grand Rapids, MI: Revell, 2004), pp. 76–77.

6. Diane Coleman, "Not Dead Yet," from testimony before the U.S. Senate Judiciary Subcommittee on the Constitution, Civil Rights and Property Rights, May 25, 2006, http://judiciary.senate.gov/print_testimony.cfm?id=1916&wit_id=5379.

Chapter 8: Poverty

1. These and the figures in the following paragraph are from U.S. Census Bureau, *Income, Poverty, and Health Insurance Coverage in the United States: 2005*. Available at www.census.gov/prod/2006pubs/p60-231.pdf.

2. Jason DeParle, *American Dream: Three Women, Ten Kids, and a Nation's Drive to End Welfare* (New York: Viking, 2004), p. 14.

3. Jim Wallis, *God's Politics: Why the Right Gets It Wrong and the Left Doesn't Get It* (San Francisco: HarperSanFrancisco, 2005), pp. 212, 214 (italics in original).

4. On marital status and poverty see U.S. Census Bureau, *Income, Poverty, and Health Insurance Coverage in the United States: 2005*, p. 14. On education and poverty see "Education" and "Education Attainment" at http://factfinder.census.gov/servlet/ACSSAFFPeople?_submenuID-people_5&_sse-on.

5. Unnamed volunteer, quoted in Roy Herron, *How Can a Christian Be in Politics? A Guide toward Faithful Politics* (Wheaton, IL: Tyndale House, 2005), p. 33.

6. See U.S. Census Bureau data, available at http://pubdb3.census.gov/macro/031995/pov/1_001.htm and http://pubdb3.census.gov/macro/032001/pov/new01_001.htm.

Chapter 9: Caring for God's Creation

1. What Would Jesus Drive? "Call to Action,"www.whatwouldjesusdrive.org/action/call.php.

2. R. Scott Rodin, "Stewardship," in Ronald J. Sider and Diane Knippers, eds., *Toward an Evangelical Public Policy* (Grand Rapids, MI: Baker Books, 2005), p. 270.

3. The World Conservation Union, also known as the International Union for the Conservation of Nature and Natural Resources, http://iucn.org/themes/ssc/red_list_2004/Extinction_media_brief_2004.pdf.

4. Steven Bouma-Prediger, *For the Beauty of the Earth* (Grand Rapids, MI: Baker Academic, 2001), p. 45.

5. Gene Edward Veith, "To Protect and Conserve," *World*, May 20, 2006, p. 30.

6. Elizabeth Arnold, "Saving the Spotted Owl," National Public Radio, August 5, 2004, www.npr.org/templates/story/story.php?storyId=3815722.

7. California Air Resources Board, www.arb.ca.gov/aqd/aqfaq.

8. John M. Broder, "Cleaner Los Angeles Air? Don't Hold Your Breath," *New York Times*, November 4, 2004.

9. For information on global warming and its extent and causes, see Sir John Houghton, "Climate Change: A Christian Challenge and Opportunity" (address, National Association of Evangelicals, March 2005); and Sir John Houghton, interview by Jim Ball (executive director of the Evangelical Environmental Network), Evangelical Environmental Network and *Creation Care* Magazine, www.creationcare.org/resources/climate.

10. Eric Chivian, letter to the editor, *New York Times*, January 6, 2007.

11. Houghton, interview by Jim Ball.

12. Houghton, interview by Jim Ball.

Chapter 10: Violations of Human Rights

1. Soon Ok Lee, International Christian Concern, "Hall of Shame 2007: The World's Ten Worst Persecutors of Christians," at www.persecution.org/suffering/pdfs/HallofShame2007.pdf. This is an excellent Web site for information on the persecution of Christians around the world. Also very helpful is the Hudson Institute's Center for Religious Freedom (http://crf.hudson.org).

2. David B. Barrett, cited in Paul Marshall, *Their Blood Calls Out* (Nashville: W Publishing, 1997), Appendix D.

3. Marshall, *Their Blood Calls Out*, Appendix D.

4. Mehdi Dibaj, quoted in Allen Hertzke, *Freeing God's Children: The Unlikely Alliance for Global Human Rights* (Lanham, MD: Rowman and Littlefield, 2004), p. 60.

5. Reena, quoted in U.S. Department of State, Office to Monitor and Combat Trafficking in Persons, "Trafficking in Persons Report," June 5, 2006, www.state.gov/g/tip/rls/tiprpt/2006/65983.htm.

6. U.S. Department of State, "Trafficking in Persons Report."

7. Kevin Bales, cited in David Batstone, *Not for Sale* (San Francisco: HarperSanFrancisco, 2007), p. 1.

8. Free the Slaves, www.freetheslaves.net.

9. Michael Gerson, "A New Social Gospel," *Newsweek*, November 13, 2006, p. 40.

10. Hertzke, *Freeing God's Children*, p. 83.

11. Walter Russell Mead, "God's Country?" *Foreign Affairs*, September–October 2006, p. 9. Available at www.foreignaffairs.org/20060901faessay85504/walter-russell-mead/god-country.html

12. Mead, "God's Country?" p. 9.

13. Hertzke, *Freeing God's Children*, p. 37.

14. See Hertzke, *Freeing God's Children*, pp. 250–57.

15. Quoted in Hertzke, *Freeing God's Children*, p. 207.

Chapter 11: Disease and Poverty in Africa

1. Nicholas Kristof, "Where Faith Thrives," *New York Times*, March 26, 2005, p. A13.

2. Philip Jenkins, *The Next Christendom: The Coming of Global Christianity* (New York: Oxford University Press, 2002), pp. 3–4.

3. Kristof, "Where Faith Thrives," A13.

4. British Commission on Africa, "Our Common Interest: Report of the Commission for Africa," 11. Available at www.commissionforafrica.org/english/report/thereport/english/11-03-05_cr_report.pdf.

5. World Bank, "Global Monitoring Report 2007." Available at www.worldbank.org/ under "Data & Research" and then "Global Monitoring Report."

6. World Bank, 1993, www.worldbank.org/afr/poverty/measuring/cross_country_en.htm.

7. King Mswati III, quoted in Amy S. Patterson, *The Politics of AIDS in Africa* (Boulder, CO: Lynne Rienner, 2006), p. 1.

8. United Nations, "2006 AIDS Epidemic Update Report," http://data.unaids.org/pub/EpiReport/2006/04-Sub-Saharan_africa_2006_EpiUpdate_eng.pdf. On the number of orphans, see www.avert.org/aidsorphans.htm.

9. Malaria No More, www.malarianomore.org/about.php (accessed January 18, 2007).

10. Isaac Mutua, "What Is That in Your Hand? Realizing Africa's Potential," *Contact*, September 2005, p. 12.

11. Mary Kortenhoven, quoted in Matt Vanden Bunte, " 'Blood Diamond' a Reality for Missionaries," *Grand Rapids Press*, January 20, 2007. Mary Kortenhoven is a missionary of the Christian Reformed Church World Relief Committee.

12. Kay Warren, quoted in Timothy C. Morgan, "Purpose Driven in Rwanda," *Christianity Today*, October 2005, 49.

13. For more information, see "The P.E.A.C.E. Plan," www.thepeaceplan.com/.

14. George W. Bush, "2003 State of the Union Address," www.whitehouse.gov/news/releases/2003/01/20030128-19.html.

15. U.S. Agency for International Development (USAID), "U.S. Overseas Loans and Grants," iii. Available at pdf.usaid.gov/pdf_docs/PNADH500.pdf.

16. Peter Okaalet, quoted in Rhoda Tse, "Faith-Based Hero: Dr. Peter Okaalet," ChristianPost.com, November 2, 2005, www.christianpost.com/article/20051102/21477.htm.

17. Patterson, *The Politics of AIDS in Africa*, p. 29.

18. The Lectionary, "Janani Luwum, Archbishop of Uganda and Martyr," www.satucket.com/lectionary/janani_luwum.htm.

19. The United Nations, "2006 AIDS Epidemic Update Report."

20. United Nations, "2006 AIDS Epidemic Update Report," p. 10.

21. Mark Galli, "Evangelical DNA and International Affairs," *Review of Faith and International Affairs* 4 (Winter 2006): 54.

22. Patterson, *The Politics of AIDS in Africa*, p. 63.

23. AVERT, "AIDS Orphans," www.avert.org/aidsorphans.htm (accessed January 18, 2007).

24. Celia W. Dugger, "Bush Celebrates Early Victories in Campaign against Malaria," *New York Times*, December 15, 2006.

25. George W. Bush, June 30, 2005. Available at www.usaid.gov/fightingmalaria/resources/pmi_fastfacts.pdf.

26. See Kimberly A. Elliott, "Agriculture and the Doha Round," Center for Global Development, www.cgdev.org/.

27. See Jubilee Debt Campaign, www.jubileedebtcampaign.org.uk/?lid=2675.

28. Jubilee Debt Campaign, www.jubileedebtcampaign.org.uk.

Chapter 12: War and Terrorism

1. Jean-Marie Colombani, "We Are All Americans Now," *Le Monde*, September 12, 2001. World Press Review, November 2001, www.worldpress.org/1101we_are_all_americans.htm.

2. James Madison, *The Federalist* (New York: Modern Library), p. 337.

3. This signed statement ran in several newspapers. See, for example, *New York Times*, June 13, 2006, A23. It is also available at www.nrcat.org/ under "Torture is a Moral Issue."

4. George W. Bush, President's Remarks at National Day of Prayer and Remembrance, National Cathedral, Washington, DC, September 2001, www.whitehouse.gov/news/releases/2001/09/20010914-2.html.

5. George W. Bush, address before the joint session of Congress, September 2001, www.whitehouse.gov/news/releases/2001/09/20010920-8.html.

Subject Index

Scripture Index

Genesis
1:1—31, 33, 148
1:27—28, 118
1:28—150
1:31—33
2:15—34
2:18—83
2:22–24—83
3:5–6—37
3:12–13—37
3:15—39
3:17—38

Exodus
15:2—194

Leviticus
19:9–10—140
23:22—140
25—192

Deuteronomy
15:11—131, 134, 145
16:18–20—48
16:20—46
24:1–4—83
30:19—114

1 Samuel
10:19—78

2 Chronicles
7:14—20

Job
38–40—33
38:7—33
41:11—148

Psalms
24:1—147
24:1–2—148
33:12—20
50:12—148
72:12–14—49
104:24—149
104:25–26—149
147:3—178

Proverbs
8:15–16—48

Isaiah
1:11–12—53
1:15—53–54
1:17—54
1:21–22—51
1:23—54
10:1–2—52
58:6–7—135
61:1—164

Amos
5:12—49, 52
5:15—52

Matthew
5:31–32—83
6:12—202
10:16—172
18:23–35—192
22:21—97
22:37–40—64
22:39—62
24:6—196
25:40—135
25:45—71

Mark
7:20–23—37

Luke
4:18—164, 168
6:28—92
6:35—92

John
19:10–11—48

Acts
2:1—83
13:2–3—83
15:1–35—83
15:40—83

222

Made in the USA
Monee, IL
24 August 2023

41590822R00125